HOLLYWOOD IN THE SEVENTIES

LES KEYSER

SAN DIEGO • NEW YORK
A. S. BARNES & COMPANY, INC.
IN LONDON:
THE TANTIVY PRESS

First Edition
Manufactured in the United States of America

For information write to:
A. S. Barnes & Company, Inc.
P.O. Box 3051
La Jolla, California 92038

The Tantivy Press
Magdalen House
136-148 Tooley Street
London, SE1 2TT, England

Library of Congress Cataloging in Publication Data

Keyser, Lester J   1943–
  Hollywood in the 70's.

  Includes index.
  1. Moving-pictures—United States.   I. Title.
PN1993.5.U6K45   1981   791.43'0973   80-26564
ISBN 0-498-02545-4

1 2 3 4 5 6 7 8 9 84 83 82 81

For Catherine

Contents

*Karen Black on Mount Lee in John Schlesinger's **THE DAY OF THE LOCUST** (1975).*

1. Goodbye, Yellow Brick Road

"What is Hollywood?
It's just a studio.
It's here today, and there tomorrow."
OTTO PREMINGER

ON VETERANS DAY in 1978, hundreds of participants in Hollywood's constant celebrity wars jammed a 22,000-square-foot tent alongside Griffith Park Observatory to witness the unveiling of a new Hollywood sign atop Mount Lee. The old sign, an advertising ploy for Hollywoodland, a real estate development that failed, had fallen into disrepair, and the image-conscious Hollywood Chamber of Commerce cajoled show-biz patrons to contribute $27,777 for each letter so that this landmark could be refurbished in honor of the seventy-fifth birthday of Hollywood's incorporation as a city. CBS was to broadcast the unveiling as part of a two-hour Hollywood Diamond Jubilee Special, and a magnificent light show complete with laser optics was planned. Torrential rains and thunderstorms came, however, and the seventy-five-dollar-a-ticket notables quickly discovered that the tent leaked and that rain-soaked Astroturf makes a sodden mess on Guccis. The promoters were unable to cover the sign because of the storm; thus there was no unveiling and no laser display.

In a decade that witnessed, according to the consensus of chroniclers, the death of the Old Hollywood and the phoenix-like rebirth of a New Hollywood, this checkered Diamond Jubilee party seems rife with ironies. All the problems at Mount Lee began, for example, when the project left the studio soundstage and sheltered backlot to pitch its behemoth tents on location.

Yet the New Hollywood is essentially a rejection of the old studio systems in favor of freelance, catch-as-catch-can, location-oriented, media-hyped projects. Even the bad weather at the Jubilee is an ironic comment on the good weather that first drew movie companies to California. (Many early filmmakers feared legal entanglements in the patent wars and found both the constant sunlight and the proximity to

1

Mexico useful.) By the Seventies, however, the Chamber of Commerce and the new celebrities all wore the same silk suits, used the same law firms and banks, and endured the same rains. The New Hollywood image is corporate, successful, subdued, and civic-minded.

And then there is the real estate sign itself, a faintly ironic suggestion of the historic reversals taking place. If the Old Hollywood had built backlots where developers wanted tract housing, the New Hollywood was watching frenzied real estate speculators convert old studios to new parking lots. Even Beverly Hills itself was being sold to the oil-rich sheiks of the Middle East. Sheik Al Fassi, for example, brought plastic flowers, garish nude statues, and a multicolored airplane beacon to a stately Beverly Hills mansion only to see his palace perish in flames of mysterious origin.

The final irony, of course, is the omnipresence of CBS at Hollywood's birthday party. Old Hollywood had seen television as an enemy, a competitor, the ugly new kid in town; New Hollywood knew much better how syndicated shows and movies kept studios open and workers employed. The big screen and little screen had slowly but surely coexisted and cooperated, and many of those present at Mount Lee that night shifted easily from one format to another. These new multimedia personalities were already speculating privately that television, the record industry, and cinema would merge in the next decade via videodiscs and videocassettes, if only the technical gremlins would not keep turning out the lights.

Perhaps the best description of the dramatic shift from the Old Hollywood to the New was provided by reporter–raconteur–scholar Richard Dyer MacCann whose 1962 text *Hollywood in Transition* (reprinted 1977) is as entertaining as it is prescient. MacCann saw four freedoms coming to Tinseltown: the freedom from the control of centralized studios, the freedom from the tyranny of the assembly line, the freedom from the domination of the domestic box office, and the freedom from censorship. Add to MacCann's emerging liberties the advent of a new audience, the vagaries of a new overheated economy, and the uncertainties of a major revolution in electronics, and one can understand some of the forces that shaped the American film industry in the Seventies.

2

By comparison, the good old days in Hollywood were much simpler. Moguls who knew the business presided over vast lots employing thousands of performers, stars, directors, producers, and craftsmen. There were writers and costumers, cooks and stuntmen, all on payroll; time clocks and regular schedules prevailed at the Dream Factory, and each week a steady flow of product went out to a well-established circuit of theaters. As critic Charles Higham so gracefully wrote in his elegiac history *Hollywood at Sunset,* audiences always knew what to expect from the "majors": Paramount provided "lightheartedness," MGM "sentimental saintliness," Warners "toughness," Twentieth Century-Fox "sophisticated gloss," Universal "pioneer briskness," and Columbia "ritziness." Things changed as America changed, however. After the Second World War, audiences fled the city for the suburbs, television provided free entertainment right in the living room or out on the patio, and the government severed studio-exhibitor links through antitrust actions. Profits became erratic and losses mounted; the major studios were in trouble. As director Stanley Kubrick observed, "the invulnerability of the majors was based on their consistent success with virtually anything they made." When virtually everything they did resulted in failure, the studios were vulnerable. For a while in the late Sixties, it looked like the last picture show might be small budget, youth-oriented films. *Easy Rider* (1969) not only challenged the industry; it threatened a stampede from Hollywood Boulevard to Taos.

Paradoxically, however, it was not long-haired dope dealers but clean-cut conservative businessmen who created the New Hollywood of the Seventies. The new decade heralded the age of multinational corporations, conglomerates, and synergism. Hollywood studios were just another set of companies and ledgers to the new acquisitions-oriented entrepreneurs. Mel Brooks captures some of the sense of the early Seventies in his hilarious spoof of the shenanigans involved in the birth of the original studios, *Silent Movie* (1976). Brooks envisions a company named Engulf and Devour taking over Sunshine Studio to put up a shopping center, a telling comment on Paramount's fate under Gulf and Western and Warner Brothers' fate with Kinney Corporation, the king of parking lots. Brooks also presents a "Big Pictures Studio" production with the revealing legend

3

"*Ars est pecunia.*" As director Brooks well knew, much of the history of Hollywood in the Seventies is a sad tale of art and money at war in an atmosphere controlled by "Engulf and Devour" Incorporated.

Conglomerates absorbed film companies for simple economic reasons. The studios, to begin with, could be bought at bargain-basement prices, especially considering the value of their real estate holdings. Director Robert Aldrich had predicted in 1968 that "the land the major studios are on will become so expensive that they will no longer be able to function where they are"; the conglomerates of the Seventies proved him right. Conglomerates also understood the value of film libraries; the product of Old Hollywood made the New Hollywood worth owning. Television needed movies badly and was willing to pay high prices. The conglomerates saw a bonanza waiting to be grabbed. Universal was absorbed by Music Corporation of America, an expert operation when it came to measuring the worth of rights and permissions, and United Artists was bought by TransAmerica Corporation, which also controlled Bank of America. And there was still that other intangible, the charisma, charm, and star quality of the studios, ready to be exploited. MGM, the home of the stars, held what foreign observers called a "clearance sale" of its props and sets in 1970, but kept its image as untarnished as possible, so that the glorious past could be exploited in its Grand Hotel, a casino operation in Las Vegas. As Frank E. Rosenfelt, the president of MGM, noted in 1979, his company "incorporated the glamor and excitement of Hollywood and the movie business into the hotel and casino operation. . . . This is truly synergism in its purest and most successful form." Glamor, excitement, incorporation, business, and success—these are the key words in the conglomerate cinema of the Seventies.

For their film operations, the conglomerates rejected the old studio model, the factory of hired hands working under autocratic bosses to create an endless flow of product, and looked instead to the example of United Artists, a company with no studio and fewer workers, organized principally to distribute features made by independent producers. Like United Artists, all the companies of the New Hollywood put great emphasis on financing and distributing; they contracted "in house" or with independents to see that product was made, usually somewhere else, away from corporate headquarters and the executive

Harold Gould as an acquisitions-happy executive from ''Engulf and Devour'' in Mel Brooks' SILENT MOVIE (1976).

Jane Fonda and James Caan in Alan J. Pakula's COMES A HORSEMAN (1978).

suites. Andrew Sarris, film critic extraordinaire of the Seventies, described this process perspicaciously in his review of *Comes a Horseman* (1978) for the *Village Voice:* "Nowadays, producers, agents, and moneymen meet indiscriminately with bankable stars, bankable directors, and bankable writers to discuss bankable projects. The 'Deal' becomes the instant 'Studio' and as soon as the Deal is either fulfilled or broken off, the Studio vanishes in the mists like Brigadoon." As Sarris notes, "One is never sure these days how a project gets started, and by whom it is propelled." The studio credits tell only who financed it and who distributed it. The real studio, the real production company, of a film like *Comes a Horseman* is, as Sarris observes, a "one shot, once-in-a-lifetime" combination of director Alan Pakula, writer Dennis Clark, producers Irwin Winkler and Robert Chartoff, players including James Caan, Jane Fonda, and Jason Robards, and "whatever agents, intermediaries, and head waiters are necessary to complete the negotiations." No wonder Tom Wolfe's infamous lady with hemorrhoids, in his essay "The Me Decade and the Third Great Awakening," felt that only one credit line should go on the screen for any movie: "Deal by. . . ."

Joan Didion aptly called the deal "the new art form" in Hollywood, as artists in the narcissistic Seventies boldly declared their fixation on profits. Individual performers mirrored the conglomerate ethic, linking screen performances, television appearances, and product endorsements with franchising operations, real estate developments, and even political campaigns. America's leading actor, Marlon Brando, who made millions for a few weeks' work on *Superman* (1978) and then sued for more, boldly declared to the readers of *Playboy* that in Hollywood, "there are no artists. We are businessmen. We're merchants." To sell their talents, actors, directors, cameramen, and practically everyone else had their own agents, managers, and personal representatives, as deals were made everywhere, and it seemed everyone was always "taking a meeting."

Woody Allen captures the hothouse atmosphere of a deal-oriented Hollywood well in his Academy Award-winning *Annie Hall* (1977). Just as soon as Allen's East Coast hero, Alvy Singer, finally reaches the West Coast, he is whisked to a cocktail and cocaine party, where one laid-back actor purrs to another about his manager, "Not only is he a good agent, but he gives great meetings." Language and logic are

6

Marlon Brando and Susannah York in Richard Donner's
SUPERMAN (1978).

further fractured in another conversation at the same party where it is explained that, in Hollywood, a notion supported by money becomes a concept and a concept supported by money is an idea.

Deals were so omnipresent in the Hollywood of the Seventies that even established commercial directors like Herbert Ross, the man responsible for *Play It Again, Sam* (1972), *Funny Lady* (1975), *The Sunshine Boys* (1975), *The Turning Point* (1977), *The Goodbye Girl* (1977), and *California Suite* (1978), never lost their nervousness. Ross told one interviewer that "We're all paranoid in film. We're afraid to leave town because somebody else will be there instead of us." No one seemed immune from dealing Hollywood style. Politicians like Julian Bond and John Lindsay, sports figures like Mohammed Ali and Ken Norton, film critics like Pauline Kael and Rex Reed, television stars like John Travolta and Henry Winkler, all heard the siren call of the megabucks of the New Hollywood. And everyone learned the same lesson Sylvester Stallone did when he made his million-to-one shot pay off in *Rocky* (1976) and *Rocky II* (1979). As Stallone so aptly put it, "Hollywood is not a town. Hollywood is a business. You don't move to Hollywood to Live. You move to Hollywood to survive, to work, to strive. It's not a place where you vacation, because the air is so thick with shattered dreams and ambitions, with energy and creativity."

So much energy and ambition goes into dealing in contemporary Hollywood that the old-guard directors like Billy Wilder complain that eighty percent of their time goes to making deals and only twenty percent to making pictures. Young director Michael Ritchie must agree, because his admirable spoof of contemporary film festivals, *An Almost Perfect Affair* (1979), ends with the lesson "It's not the film. . . . It's the deal." The Hollywood one-liner for the Seventies might well be the popular Polo Lounge canard: "Blessed are the deal makers for they shall inherit the industry."

Deals determine what goes on screen in the Seventies, and sometimes the changes in a project from conception to execution are sweeping. Paul Schrader, the hottest screenwriter of the Seventies, for example, described the evolution of one of the decade's finest films, *Taxi Driver* (1976), in a lengthy Spring 1975 *Film Comment* interview. The first plan for *Taxi Driver,* Schrader reports, was to do it with Robert Mulligan and Jeff Bridges, an idea Schrader thought did

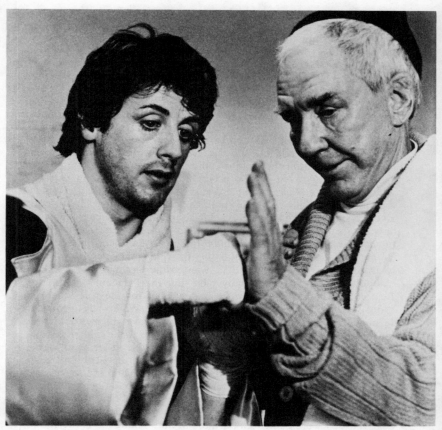

Sylvester Stallone and Burgess Meredith in John Avildsen's ROCKY (1976).

not make any sense, but which tempted him because it was a commercially viable deal. He knew that studios would buy this project, arrange the financing, handle the distribution, and the film would be made. Schrader held out for a while, however, and actor Robert De Niro and director Martin Scorsese became interested in a deal; they offered to do the film at reduced salaries with larger profit participation. Despite the fact that financing this package was a smaller burden to a studio, the proposed deal did not become commercial until the successes of De Niro in *Godfather II* (1974) and Scorsese with *Alice Doesn't Live Here Anymore* (1975). As Schrader recalls the negotiations, no studio really wanted to make *Taxi Driver,* but "we were offering them too good a deal." *Taxi Driver* was made then only when the deal was an offer the studios could not refuse.

The deals involved in the production of the Academy Award-winning *Coming Home* (1978) also garnered some publicity that sheds a good deal of light on power politics in contemporary Hollywood. Every project must have a "pre-sold" look, the air of success, and the appeal of a star who means big box office before the majors will help finance the production. When *Coming Home* was first discussed, Jon Voight was tentatively chosen to play the role which eventually went to Bruce Dern. Voight, however, wanted the larger role of Luke, a characterization that eventually won him the Academy Award for Best Actor, but Voight knew he had to fight for the role when he "took a meeting" with star Jane Fonda, writer Waldo Salt, producer Jerome Hellman, and director Hal Ashby. Jon Voight had not had a big hit in a while, and thus he was not bankable. As he told interviewers, "I felt down at the bottom of the totem pole in terms of viable commercial personalities, and I was. In other words, I couldn't get a film made." For all the other celebrities to invite him in the package was, Voight knew, a gift, yet at his meeting he also felt he had to fight to enlarge his participation and to upgrade his role. The role of Luke was designed for a "viable" star, and, as Voight himself acknowledged, "they were going to have a tough time selling me to the studio even with Jane's name." Voight took his meeting successfully, of course, and the studio bought the package. Nevertheless, Voight's Academy Award-winning portrayal might not have been a bankable deal, if the other elements in the package had not been so attractive.

Robert DeNiro in Martin Scorsese's TAXI DRIVER (1976).

Jon Voight and Jane Fonda in Hal Ashby's COMING HOME (1978).

Prior success at the box office, a "track record" provides the key to power in movie deal making; in Hollywood today, you are "only as good as your last film." Performers like Jack Nicholson, Barbra Streisand, and Robert Redford write their own deals for all intents and purposes, working only on projects that interest them artistically, politically, or financially. A box-office draw like Clint Eastwood, reigning king of the macho circuit with Burt Reynolds, can force Paramount to pay him three million dollars in advance for films like *Escape from Alcatraz* (1978) against a fifteen percent share of worldwide gross receipts, a deal that should net him over ten million dollars. John Travolta and Olivia Newton-John both had substantial interests in *Grease* (1978), and rumor has it that Alec Guinness' stint as Ben (Obi Wan) Kenobi in *Star Wars* (1977) made him one of the world's richest actors since he worked for a participation in the gross.

Actors are, however, no longer protected and developed by the studios; their careers are in their own hands, and a few flops can send them careening back to obscurity. Elliott Gould, a fixture in early Seventies features like *M*A*S*H* (1970), *Getting Straight* (1970), and *Little Murders* (1971), found himself overexposed by mid-decade, while Gene Hackman, the hero of *The French Connection* (1971), turned down major roles in *Network* (1976), *Jaws* (1975), *Close Encounters of the Third Kind* (1977), and *One Flew Over the Cuckoo's Nest* (1975) with little rhyme or reason for his decisions. Freedom could both enrich a career and diminish it.

Directors in the Seventies also discovered the joys and perils of liberty. Whiz kids like George Lucas moved from film school shorts to small productions like *THX1138* (1970) for American Zoetrope and then to major studio efforts like *American Graffiti* (1973), which made millions for Universal, and *Star Wars* (1977), which might make billions eventually for Twentieth Century-Fox. Lucas is now obviously his own boss; the studio and money managers need him more than he needs them. By the end of the decade, he was already wealthy and independent enough to enter joint ventures with the Robert Stigwood Organization, a key force in both music and cinema.

Other talented people in Hollywood also enjoyed new liberties in this world of freelance dealing. After years of struggle, embittered battles with unions and seniority rules, court cases, and other such chicanery, a new group of cinematographers gained access to Ameri-

Robert Shaw, Steven Spielberg, and Roy Scheider filming JAWS (1975).

can screens. Armed with the new Panavision cameras, improved film stocks, and sophisticated lighting equipment, this new breed of cinematographer generated many stunning visual achievements. Films in the Seventies frequently bedazzled and always forced their audience to see in new ways. Cameramen like Haskell Wexler (*The Conversation*, 1974; *Bound for Glory*, 1976; *Coming Home*, 1978), Gordon Willis (*Klute*, 1971; *The Godfather*, 1972; *All the President's Men*, 1976; *Manhattan*, 1979), William Fraker (*One Flew Over the Cuckoo's Nest*, 1975; *Looking for Mr. Goodbar*, 1977; *Heaven Can Wait*, 1978), Vilmos Zsigmond (*McCabe and Mrs. Miller*, 1971; *the Long Goodbye*, 1973; *Close Encounters of the Third Kind*, 1977), and Laszlo Kovacs (*Five Easy Pieces*, 1970; *Shampoo*, 1975; *New York, New York*, 1972) were crucial participants in any artistic success, as were editors like Dede Allen (*Little Big Man*, 1970; *Serpico*, 1973; *Dog Day Afternoon*, 1975; *Slap Shot*, 1977) and Verna Fields (*American Graffiti*, 1973; *The Sugarland Express*, 1974; *Jaws*, 1975). The right combination of talent assured a project would be made, that the execution would be professional, and that the distribution would be worldwide. As always, however, Hollywood was still a great crap shot, a desperate gamble that the final product would find an audience.

To minimize the chance of losses and to maximize the opportunity for profits, the film companies of the Seventies developed new relationships with each other, with independent producers, and with exhibitors. No longer overburdened with the costs and responsibilities of backlots and studios, film companies found it easier to cooperate with each other on major products than to compete. Conglomerates were all for economies of scale, so the decade saw one major coproduction after another. Warner Brothers and Twentieth Century-Fox, for example, when they discovered they had similar projects on the drawing boards, merged them in the gigantic production of *The Towering Inferno* (1974); United Artists and Universal cooperated on *Yanks* (1979), and MGM and Warners jointly produced *The Goodbye Girl* (1977). Sometimes, in fact, it was hard to tell one studio from another, as even executives found the musical chairs of deal making and private production teams irresistible. When the executives at United Artists tired of interference from higher-ups in TransAmerica, their conglomerate, they formed Orion Pictures and

15

quickly made a deal with Warner Brothers, which included exclusive rights to distribute Orion pictures like *A Little Romance* (1979). Similarly, when Alan Ladd, Jr., Jay Kanter, and Gareth Wigan tired of Twentieth Century-Fox's financial strictures, they formed their own production company and arranged the distribution of their films through Warner Brothers.

By decade's end, the old majors were shifting more and more energies to distribution; the old monopoly of production was crushed, but a new hegemony on distribution was growing. The majors had the capital, the contacts, the experience, and the muscle to tap both the international and domestic markets. They were able to work with independents like Mel Simon and Stephen Friedman just as they had worked earlier in the decade with tax shelter groups like Persky-Bright and Devon. One set of investment-tax loopholes, not closed by Congress till midway through the decade, allowed shrewd accountants, professionals, and speculators to pump almost 150 million dollars into film and related projects with the bulk of the real cost borne by the American government. Major films like *The Man Who Would Be King* (1973), *The Front* (1976), and *The Missouri Breaks* (1976) all involved some tax shelter arrangements. All the tax shelter deals that produced footage suitable for distribution found those groups confronting the majors, who offered contracts demanding even larger percentages of the gross than their normal one-third for domestic distribution and forty percent for foreign distribution. Sometimes the majors squeezed independents so hard that the independents tried to open films in a few cities on their own to give themselves leverage on a better deal. A good example of this is Mel Simon's gamble with Stanley Kramer's classy tale of a priest accused of murdering a nun, *The Runner Stumbles* (1979), a first-rate production hampered by the fact that none of its principals—Dick Van Dyke, Kathleen Quinlan, or Maureen Stapleton—were bankable.

The majors also managed to squeeze exhibitors more effectively than ever in the Seventies. The number of screens in America had remained fairly constant throughout the decade, with around ten thousand "four wall" operations and around three thousand drive-ins, but the number of films available had shrunk considerably compared with the supply in earlier eras. This "product shortage" enabled distributors to demand large advances and guarantees, longer

The Sirens of Poppy Street in Sidney Lumet's THE WIZ (1978).

runs, and gargantuan percentages of box-office profits. First-run profits were often split according to formulas giving ninety percent or more to the distributor and ten percent or less to the exhibitor after the house "nut" had been deducted. Many small showmen were no longer really in the movie business; they were popcorn salesmen.

The majors actually forced "blind bidding" on most exhibitors, so that a deal was all arranged even before the local theater owners had seen a single still, let alone a preview of the film they were committed to show. Films like *The Wiz* (1978), *Exorcist II* (1977), and *Sergeant Pepper's Lonely Hearts Club Band* (1978) owe some of their grosses to the fact they were "blind bid." Exhibitors had so little power vis-à-vis distributors, in fact, that they approached state legislatures to pass antiblind-bidding statutes; Southern lawmakers did so in a number of states with the result that real "first run" product rarely entered the South until well after its national release. Several northern states that generated substantial film rentals also outlawed blind bidding, and by the end of the decade, a large coalition of state lawmakers and irate exhibitors was forming to battle the studios. Antiblind-bidding short films were also shown in major theaters in an attempt to generate public support.

Things were changing so fast during the Seventies that all the old alignments had disintegrated. Producers, distributors, and exhibitors behaved as if they were friends sometimes and deadly enemies other times. Scandals emerged occasionally, but were quickly forgotten until the Begelman affair at Columbia focused all eyes on the alleged tricky bookkeeping, inflated expenses, and devious business practices of the new film companies. If the decade began with the worry that hippies and anarchists might subvert the industry, the decade ended under a cloud of doubt concerning exactly what conglomerate capitalists, who group publisher William Targ so gleefully describes in his autobiography *Indecent Pleasures* as a coven of "megalomaniacs, financial katzenjammers, packagers, and wheeler-dealers," had done to American film finances.

All investigations of Hollywood were complicated by the "internationalization" of the film business. Hollywood really had little to do with geography and national boundaries; well over forty percent of the gross receipts of Seventies films released by major studios came from foreign markets. Hollywood film companies and their affiliates and subsidiaries were just as multinational as the conglomerates that owned them. The global village was the marketplace the majors wanted to control. All Hollywood trembled when, in May 1979, the Federal Trade Commission began the largest investigation of the film business since the antitrust hearings of the Forties "to determine if Hollywood movie makers are banding together to exclude independent distributors from the extremely lucrative foreign market."

Film companies in America were more than just exporting films, however. There were international co-productions, like the ill-fated Russian–American adaptation of *The Blue Bird* (1976) with Elizabeth Taylor, Jane Fonda, Ava Gardner, and Cicely Tyson, directed by George Cukor. There were special "national" production companies in countries that subsidized films, and there were productions like William Peter Blatty's *The Ninth Configuration* (1979), independently financed with profits from Coca Cola "blocked" in foreign nations and distributed by United Film Distributors, a subsidary of the United Artists theater circuit (not related to the United Artists distribution company).

All this international activity invited competition, of course, and a "seventh" major emerged on the American scene, the British-based E.M.I., which invested over thirty million dollars in 1977 to develop film projects in America, including the award-winning *The Deer Hunter* (1978). Sir Lew Grade's I.T.C. also managed to corral John Sturges for *The Eagle Has Landed* (1978), Peter Hyams for *Capricorn One* (1978), and Michael Winner for *Firepower* (1979), all multimillion dollar undertakings aimed at both the world market and American screens. E.M.I. and I.T.C. formed Associated Film Distribution (AFD) to give these British companies maximum clout in the marketplace.

The line between foreign film and Hollywood products became very hazy, both financially and artistically, in the Seventies. Milos Forman, a principal in the Czech New Wave, made three of the decade's most interesting American films, *Taking Off* (1971), *One Flew Over the Cuckoo's Nest* (1975), and *Hair* (1979). Antonioni, the intellectual's favorite, offered *Zabriskie Point* (1970) to a puzzled nation; Bertolucci, the New York Film Festival's favorite director, worked with Jill Clayburgh on *La Luna* (1979); Louis Malle captured turn-of-the-century New Orleans in his *Pretty Baby* (1978); Roger Vadim directed

Pretty Maids All in a Row (1971); and expatriate Ingmar Bergman found himself working for Dino De Laurentiis, himself an expatriate based in Los Angeles, on *The Serpent's Egg* (1978).

American talent also gravitated to foreign productions. In surprising choices, Ingmar Bergman thought Elliott Gould was just perfect for *The Touch* (1971), and Federico Fellini saw the ideal *Casanova* (1976) in that Canadian-turned-American leftist, Donald Sutherland. Dennis Hopper rebuilt his career in Wim Wenders' *An American Friend* (1977), while Jack Nicholson risked his popularity in Antonioni's *The Passenger* (1974).

National borders just could not contain production needs, distribution patterns, nor fame and celebrity in the Seventies. The world was getting smaller and Hollywood was growing larger every minute. Even during the travails of his *Apocalypse Now* (1979), *wunderkind* Francis (Ford) Coppola felt driven to underwrite the distribution of Werner Herzog's *Kaspar Hauser* in America, to produce Wim Wenders' *Hammett,* and to exhibit *Our Hitler–A Film From Germany,* written, produced, and directed by Hans-Jurgen Syberburg.

Hollywood died and was reborn in the Seventies. What had been a one-industry town spread its influence worldwide, making all the globe its soundstage and theater. In the words of Richard Dyer Mac-Cann, Hollywood is "no longer a geographical expression. It is a state of mind operating worldwide. It is a starlet at Cannes and a producer on location in Rome." The lights on Mount Lee no longer point the way to a piece of real estate; they symbolize instead a Hollywood that is here, there, and everywhere.

2. Higher and Higher

*And as we made the film in the jungles of the
Philippines, our own experience began to reflect
the American experience in Vietnam. We had
access to too much money, too much
equipment; we built villages in the jungle and the
weather destroyed them, and we went insane.
Eventually I realized that I was not making the
movie. The movie was making itself—or the
jungle was making it for me.*
FRANCIS (FORD) COPPOLA on *Apocalypse Now*

THE BANNER HEADLINE of *Variety,* January 10, 1979, brought
substantial holiday cheer to everyone in Hollywood with its bold
proclamation: "Film B.O. Doubles Over 7 Year Span." Even when
adjusted for inflation, the multibillion dollar grosses of 1978 and 1979
seemed to signal some fat years ahead for what once was conceived of
as a dying business. The euphoria of the late Seventies led the nor-
mally cautious William Chaikin, president of Avco Embassy, to de-
clare in a cryptically worded hyperbole that "more people are paying
more money to go to more good movies than at any time in the recent
past." Actually, American weekly film attendance in the Seventies
fluctuated from a low of fifteen million to a high of approximately
twenty million paid admissions, a total about one-half the audience of the early Sixties and one-fifth the trade of the late Forties. The
new Seventies audiences did pay much more, however, and they were
young, affluent, educated, and committed to movies. The so-called
"film generation" was monopolizing the theaters, and studios learned
from market analysts that they had to cater to a clientele three-quar-
ters of whom were between the ages of twelve and .twenty-nine.
American cinema in the Seventies embodied the hippie dictum: "You
can't trust anyone over thirty."

Motion Picture Association of America statistics also showed that
those with some college education went to movies much more frequently than their contemporaries and that frequent moviegoers

purchased over ninety percent of all tickets sold. Television had stolen the old audience with its aptly named broadcasts; the new audience of Seventies cinema was a narrow segment of the population, a segment, however, which controlled the largest percentage of what economists wistfully call "discretionary income." Conglomerate policymakers were equally wistful about the concentration of "discretionary and disposable income" in the hands of its loyal ticket buyers; if one could just sell the film, the film could then sell a whole line of fashions, toys, books, tee shirts, records, posters, and other franchised goods.

Commenting on the emergence of this new affluent and restless audience, Herbert J. Gans speculated in his perceptive classic *Popular Culture and High Culture* that ethnic, religious, and place differences were disappearing so rapidly in American society that "the major sources of subcultural variety are increasingly those of age and class." Applying some of Gans's insights to the film industry, critic–sociologist J. C. Jarvis, in his *Movies as Social Criticism*, hit on what appears to be the Rosetta Stone clarifying the confusing hieroglyphics of box-office success in the Seventies: ". . . the movies are freer than a hidebound, home-centered, middle-class medium like television to explore the extremities of human experience, and they are hence more interesting to adolescents who are still, after all, exploring the possibilities and limits of experience." In the "All Time Film Rental Champions" listed by *Variety* on January 2, 1979, fully sixteen of the top twenty films were Seventies productions, and nineteen were from the mid-Sixties or later. Inflation had much to do with this disproportionate showing, but so also did contemporary Hollywood's penchant for mind-boggling super-extravaganzas, extraordinary adventures that pushed audiences to the "limits of experience" and beyond. There was little hidebound, home-centered, or even middle class in the intergalactic fantasies of *Star Wars* (1977), the unearthly watery horrors of *Jaws* (1975), the mythic corridors of power in *The Godfather* (1972), the nostalgic escape of *Grease* (1978), or the demons of *The Exorcist* (1973).

Clearly, young American filmgoers wanted to fly far from Watergate, Vietnam, and the energy crisis, far from crime in the streets, austerity, and pollution in vibrant Technicolor, Panavision, quadrophonic films. The winners in the Hollywood of the Seventies were

Carrie Fisher, Chewbacca (Peter Mayhew), and Harrison Ford in George Lucas'
STAR WARS (1977).

the films that could tune out the static of impeachment hearings, summit conferences, and seminars on the urban crisis. Box-office winners in the Seventies took audiences "higher and higher" into *Close Encounters of the Third Kind* (1977), further and further into the mysteries of *The Deep* (1977); films succeeded that warmed the audience up to a *Saturday Night Fever* (1977), let them be the *One* [who] *Flew Over the Cuckoo's Nest* (1975), catapulted them down the highway of *Smokey and the Bandit* (1977), and promised them they, too, could go fifteen rounds, the whole distance, with *Rocky* (1976). For a young, energetic, and curious audience craving vivid experiences, Hollywood delivered in the Seventies with wide-screen, 70-mm, six-track Dolby stereo clarity.

No Seventies film took audiences higher or further than *Star Wars,* George Lucas' trip to "a long time ago in a galaxy far, far away." The first large-scale invitational screenings of *Star Wars* in New York City gave Twentieth Century-Fox a clear indication of the phenomenon Lucas had created. Spontaneous applause welcomed the legend receding into space of the title sequence, and the clapping did not let up for two hours. Exclamations and "oh's" and "ah's" greeted virtually every sequence, but especially the footage of the intergalactic bar and the pinball-machine-like dog fights. This noise on Broadway quickly became a boom on Wall Street as Fox's shares climbed steadily in value. All this furor was rather disconcerting for Lucas who was quite out of sorts during the shooting of the film, fearful that the project was so big he could not control it. He kept reminding associates that he was a craftsman, a filmmaker, and "not a general," though a general was sorely needed to handle the logistics on the ten million dollar project. Four years in the making, mostly in England, *Star Wars* moves with the speed of light, never giving its audiences a chance to catch their breath. There is always a new marauder just over the horizon; the little vacuum cleaner that buzzes, Artoo Detoo, and the prissy See Threepio, for example, are kidnapped by Jawas in an eerie sequence. And Luke Skywalker (Mark Hamill) is almost killed on Tatooine; his family is wiped out in a sequence for which production designer John Barry owes a great deal to *The Searchers*. Han Solo (Harrison Ford) and Chewbacca (Peter Mayhew) have to blast dramatically into hyperspace to escape annihilation. Imperial troopers seem omnipresent even if they are a trifle stiff and chronically stupid,

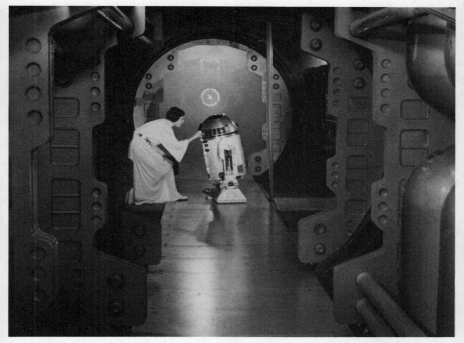

Carrie Fisher gives Artoo Detoo (Kenny Baker) the critical message in STAR WARS.

while Lord Darth Vader (David Prowse, with the voice of James Earl Jones) and his torture devices seem more than a match for Princess Leia (Carrie Fisher).

The battle lines in *Star Wars* are always crystal clear; it is black confronting white, Imperial trooper against Jedi warrior, and the "Force" frequently seems a little difficult to summon, like a genie that does not want to come out of the lamp. Ben "Obi Wan" Kenobi is paternal yet mysteriously devious, disappearing at all the critical moments to allow his spiritual children to forge their own destiny. Lucas has, by his own admission, created a classic fairy tale in the form of a space epic long on heroics; he intended his film, Lucas told interviewers, for a generation growing up without fairy tales; his target audience, he confided, was fourteen years old or younger.

Lucas' curious mixture of samurai spiritualism, Second World War heroics, Tarzan-like antics, and sets redolent of the Wild West generated so much box-office excitement that in many areas of the United States the number of tickets sold exceeded the population. *Star Wars* was a celebration, a social affair, a collective dream; and people came again and again, dragging their friends and families with them. A new Seventies phenomenon was being reenacted; like *Jaws* and *The Exorcist, Star Wars* had become one of the required experiences in life. Audiences came not just because they wanted to; they came because, in a real sense, they had to. *Star Wars* was a film that everyone had seen and was talking about, yet it was more than a matter of keeping up with the Joneses, or sharing in jokes at social gatherings, or understanding the allusions to *Star Wars* and the spoofs on television; *Star Wars* and the other blockbusters of the Seventies became events in and of themselves. To share in the history of the era, one had to experience them as cultural rites of passage.

Many, in fact, needed mementoes of their participation in *Star Wars*. By retailers' estimates, over 300 million dollars worth of *Star Wars* paraphernalia had been sold by 1980, and the market was building in anticipation of Chapter Two in the chronicle, *The Empire Strikes Back*.

Sequels were yet another Seventies phenomenon. Anything that was successful seemed worth doing again, and something as successful as *Star Wars* could enjoy annual reincarnations. Sequels were presold commodities. *The Empire Strikes Back* (1980) had over twenty-six million dollars in guarantees from American exhibitors a year before the film even opened, ensuring, as Peter Myers, vice-president of production for Fox, noted gleefully, that it "will be in profit when it opens." Such were the economics of blockbusters Hollywood-style when marketing wizards took over.

The history of Seventies Hollywood is, in large part, a chronicle of super-productions presold via massive advertising campaigns and then carefully distributed to realize every possible dollar of profit. Jack Valenti, president of MPAA, was quick to tell potential film-makers about the virtues of "sequential marketing," the seeming salvation of producers. Films could generate income in exclusive first runs, massive neighborhood engagements on showcase, long subruns, and theatrical rereleases. Then come sales to pay television and cable; then exhibition agreements with national networks and local stations, as well as rentals to nontheatrical users like airlines, hotels, and schools. Finally there are potential profits from videocassettes and videodiscs. Valenti estimated that real blockbusters might generate substantial revenues for three or four decades. A. Alan Friedberg, president of an organization of theater operators, the most beleaguered segment of the industry, took a shorter view of the producers' situation when he noted that "because of improved marketing techniques, box-office potential and ancillary rights revenues, it's a rarity for a film company to lose money on film projects." By decade's end, Wall Street analysts agreed with this assessment, and Merrill, Lynch, Pierce, Fenner, and Smith was so bullish it announced the formation of a film-financing syndicate with a potential operating fund of eighty million dollars.

New marketing strategies and conditions were largely responsible for projects like Richard Donner's mammoth reworking of the life of the perennial champion of comic strips, *Superman* (1978), an Alexander and Ilya Salkind production that lured Gene Hackman to the role of Lex Luthor, bought Marlon Brando's presence as the supernal Jor-El, and transformed unknown Christopher Reeve into the most sought-after body in the disco circuit.

The fact that this *Superman,* which cost between fifty and seventy million dollars to make, was not very good somehow seemed secondary, considering the media hype: the blitz of stories in *Time* and *Newsweek*; the eight or ten books Warner Brothers generated through

Christopher Reeve and Margot Kidder in Richard Donner's SUPERMAN (1978).

its affiliates, including a quiz book, a portfolio of oil paintings inspired by the film, some cut-out books, a book of blueprints of the movie's sets and props, and the *Great Superman Book,* a comprehensive encyclopedia of "everything you need to know about Superman, the product of seven years' research"; and the hosiery, toys, underwear, shirts, linens, and other paraphernalia that flooded the stores of America. Superman was the epitome of supersell; the film was secondary.

Director Donner actually has at least three widely disparate films on his hands in *Superman* since the diverse writing talents of Mario Puzo, David Newman, Tom Mankiewicz, and Robert Benton never quite fuse into a coherent script. The least-effective sequences are on Krypton; the crystal palace effects here, echoed in the later interview with the hologram of Jor-El, may be true to the best estimates of where chip technology will lead, but they are too solemn, brittle, and cold for an adventure movie. The sequels to *Superman*, work on which was part of the original shooting (a ploy the Salkinds also used on their Musketeer epics directed by Richard Lester), will develop the story of the villainous exiles from Krypton and may or may not reveal more of Brando's multimillion dollar performance, depending on the producers' willingness to pay his share of the gross.

The second sequence of the original *Superman,* set in rural America, is a slight improvement on Krypton, though the orchestrated panorama and folksy, populist patriotism just does not prepare an audience for the entertaining, glossy, pop-art urban sequences that follow. When Clark Kent finally gets to Metropolis, a thinly disguised New York, *Superman* flies, and Margot Kidder as Lois Lane almost steals the show from the man in tights. Their quasiromantic interludes, replete with amusingly corny sexual double entendres, are delectable. Lois at one point eyes Superman up and down and asks, "You do, don't you?" After a pregnant pause, she adds, "Eat, I mean." Superman has his own awkward moments explaining his X-ray vision to the suddenly modest Lois, and the shots of Clark Kent confronting the new open phone stands in Metropolis, devoid as they are of any booth to change in, are real showstoppers. The courtship in *Superman*, the clumsy schizophrenia of Clark Kent and his costumed alter ego, and the smug comments on sexual liberation provide just the comic perspective to make the clowning and high camp of Valerie

Perrine as Eve Teschmacher and Gene Hackman as Lex Luthor enjoyable.

The music that John Williams composed for *Superman* also did much to sustain the proper mood, but it is his masterful work on *Jaws* (1975), *Star Wars* (1977), *Close Encounters of the Third Kind* (1977), and *Dracula* (1979) that made him the most influential musical composer of the decade and the logical successor to Arthur Fiedler as conductor of the Boston Pops. In *Jaws,* the film that exploited the newly discovered summer audience in 1975, Williams' music and Verna Fields's editing combine to make the audience think they see more than they do and to force them to worry about things they cannot see.

Jaws relies on subconscious fears about deep ocean waters to mesmerize and manipulate its audience. The opening sequences, with teenagers gathered on the beach at night and an adventurous Chrissie (Susan Blacklinie) off for a nude swim only to be trapped in a churning sea of her own blood and then silently swallowed up by unseen terror, have few parallels in modern cinema; like the famous shower scene in *Psycho,* they will haunt a whole generation. No trip to the seashore now ever lacks its nervous shark jokes.

Director Steven Spielberg provides in *Jaws* both the victim's perspective and the shark's view, doubling the horror of anticipation created by Williams' inventive score. Adrift at sea with a strange trinity of science (personified by an ichthyologist, Matt Hooper [Richard Dreyfuss]), experience (embodied in almost Ahab-like grandeur by a fisherman with a Henry James name, Qùint [Robert Shaw]), and reason (encapsulated in the noble though quite weary and human sheriff, Brody [Roy Scheider]), audiences are forced to confront not only Bruce the mechanical shark but also John Milius' harrowing story of the Indianapolis and the sharks that greeted the tragic voyage of the first thermonuclear device. Reason, experience, and science are all sorely tested and wounded when the primitive is aroused. No one confronting the large open jaws, the boundless appetite, and the unreasoning destruction of the shark can be complacent, except the greedy merchants of Amity who favor a continuation of business as usual. Steven Spielberg has astutely noted that the shark in *Jaws* "dictates all the shots"; director of photography, Bill Butler, does everything he can to show how long its body is, while Spielberg

Bruce in JAWS. (1975).

31

emphasizes how stealthy and unpredictable its approach is and how massive its powers and appetites are.

No wonder a new mechanical shark, Bruce 2, was back in the water just as quickly as possible in *Jaws 2* (1978), another summer special guaranteed to hype popcorn sales in every little seashore community like Amity Beach. Again it's the teenagers who are most threatened; just when they get away from the adults and one of them loosens her bikini top, another monster shark attacks. Roy Scheider, looking a little older, wiser, and more paternal, manages to kill the shark alone this time. Director Jeannot Szwarc told interviewers *Jaws 2* was "a manipulation of the audience in the best sense of the term." Szwarc worked, he admitted, "a lot with graphs. I always put the scenes in almost mathematical terms—highs, lows," seeking the "melody of the film."

Steven Spielberg, meanwhile, was off preparing his own brand of cinematic music, *Close Encounters of the Third Kind* (1977), another blockbuster designed to carry the earthbound off to new dimensions; instead of deep water, Spielberg was pondering the skies. *Close Encounters* actually just reverses the normal meet-the-monsters-from-the-moon genre, speculating instead that some luminescent, wonderful, peaceful humanoid aliens have already visited Earth, taken Earthlings aboard their immense mothership, and now want to establish fuller communications.

Spielberg weaves around this intrinsically simple material innovative visions of the nocturnal acrobatics of UFO's, hilarious images of life in the suburbs, and chilling portraits of governmental red tape and secrecy; the aliens break through all the interference, however, with telepathic messages and a haunting musical language. Spielberg managed to shoot only about three quarters of his original script, and the fact that *Close Encounters* ends just as Roy Neary (Richard Dreyfuss) prepares to depart from Earth leaves much room for further spectacular encounters. It will be difficult, however, to match or excel the special effects so masterfully mounted in *Close Encounters* by Douglas Trumball, who had worked earlier on Stanley Kubrick's classic, *2001* (1968), and who had directed *Silent Running* (1971), scripted in part by Michael Cimino, starring Bruce Dern, and featuring songs by Joan Baez and an original score by Peter Schickele. *Silent Running,* an inventive space adventure with an ecological focus, was one of the most interesting but least popular films of 1972.

The final encounter in CLOSE ENCOUNTERS OF THE THIRD KIND (1977).

The most popular film of 1972, the "best" picture of the year, *The Godfather* was a blockbuster based on the novel by Mario Puzo, who claimed he had "never met a real honest-to-god gangster," and directed by a fledgling director, Francis Ford Coppola, whose earlier films, *You're a Big Boy Now* (1967), *Finian's Rainbow* (1968), *Dementia 13* (1962), and *The Rain People* (1969), suggested his *métier* might be failed musicals and obscure personal projects. Paramount Pictures budgeted two and one-half million dollars for *The Godfather* and planned to set the action in modern St. Louis to avoid the cost of period reconstruction. Coppola had a different vision, however, and though he was threatened with dismissal on an almost daily basis, he demanded that Marlon Brando play Don Vito Corleone and Al Pacino play Michael, that footage be shot in Sicily, and that everything be done in period. As Puzo saw it, Coppola fought the battle for the integrity of the movie, and the writer publicly declared that *The Godfather* is really Coppola's movie: "It's my book, but the big thing is standing up against the studios."

Director Sidney Pollack defined Coppola's achievement quite eloquently: "*The Godfather* isn't a 1930s gangster movie but a 1930s certainty rethought." Coppola's tale of the Corleones from 1945 to 1955 provides a series of privileged moments, almost miraculous performances, and truly inspired directorial touches. Marlon Brando, who refused the Oscar for his role, employs his raspy shallow voice, swollen cheeks, and lumbering gait to draw everyone into the dark universe he finally relinquishes to his heir. His first lament to a supplicant that had he come sooner, as a "gentleman with honor," the insult would already be avenged, his endless deals that cannot be refused, his reactions to the bungled assassination attempt, and his *tour de force* death scene, nodding gently among the tomatoes, are career landmarks. Nothing Brando does, however, dims the intensity of Al Pacino as Michael nor overshadows James Caan's impetuous gestures as the short-tempered Sonny.

Coppola intertwines these confident performances with a wealth of well-realized incidents. The severed horse's head soaking bed sheets in blood, Clemenza's spaghetti cooking, the parlays and betrayals in restaurants, Sonny's gory murder, the ceremonial hugging and laying on of hands, and the overblown wedding are photographed exquisitely by Gordon Willis and underscored by Nino Rota's forceful melodies;

Robert Duvall, Tere Livrano, John Cazale, Gianni Russo, Talia Shire, Morgana King, Marlon Brando, James Caan, Julie Gregg, and Jeannie Linero in THE GODFATHER (1972).

35

Crime and Capitalism in Francis Ford Coppola's THE GODFATHER (1972).

Al Pacino and Diane Keaton in THE GODFATHER (1972).

all these scenes prepare the way for Coppola's dramatic conclusion, a bizarre yet effective juxtaposition of infant baptism and a gangland baptism of blood, the capstone of one of the decade's most fully realized artistic achievements.

Coppola created a popular masterpiece in *The Godfather*, and he improves on it in *The Godfather, Part II*, which two years later was also declared "best picture" as well as garnering Oscars for "best director" (Coppola), "best screenplay" (Coppola and Puzo), "best supporting actor" (Robert De Niro), and "best musical score" (Nino Rota). *The Godfather, Part II* offers a frame, a context for its predecessor, limning two separate but related histories spanning three generations: one tracing Vito Corleone's youth, the murder of his family in Sicily, his lonely immigration, and his rise in the mob; and the other picturing the bloody machinations, the deals, intrigues, lies, and betrayals of his son Michael, the new Don of the Corleone clan. In *The Godfather, Part II* Coppola hammers hard at his pet thesis, expanding his metaphor of crime and capitalism; in Coppola's opinion, "the Mafia is no different from any other big, greedy, profit-making corporation in America." The Corleone saga is, in Coppola's hands, a fitting history lesson for America in the decade of its bicentennial. Michael Corleone is the consummate corporation man with a real respect for family, tradition, possessions, loyalty, and expediency. And Pacino's performance as Michael Corleone is a textbook in restraint, making his incredible explosion when he discovers Kay's abortion all the more horrifying.

The Godfather, Part III, with a script by Dean Riesner based on a Mario Puzo original story, was in the planning stages in the Seventies, with rumors circulating that the number one sex symbol and celebrity of the decade, John Travolta, whose superhits, *Grease* (1978) and *Saturday Night Fever* (1977), established his appeal to young movie goers, had been approached as a possible lead, a successor to Brando and Pacino.

Travolta's meteoric rise to eminence in the Seventies was as much a Cinderella story as Tony Manero's transformations in *Saturday Night Fever*, a frenzied look at the disco scene based on Nik Cohen's article for *New York* magazine, directed by John Badham, and produced by Robert Stigwood, the music impresario. Centered at the 2001 disco, a splashy fantasy land with lighted floors, radiant mirrors, and overdressed revelers, *Saturday Night Fever* contrasts Tony's workaday life in Bay Ridge, Brooklyn, with the freedom, vibrancy, and animal sexuality he feels once each week when he blows his pay dancing the night away on center stage at 2001. Tony is smothered by family, church, and his retarded friends; Bay Ridge offers only boredom, confinement, repression, mindless violence, and tawdry gang bangs. Over the water, a subway ride away, is Manhattan, a challenging and frightening universe that Tony must discover or die.

Travolta is a natural as Tony; his peculiar features, flamboyant hair, and athletic dancing make audiences believe that this inarticulate, stunted clotheshorse, who spends hours before his mirror preening, idolizes Bruce Lee, and agonizes over winning a dance contest, has the inner strength to grow up, keep Stephanie (Karen Lynn Gorney) as a friend, and face the real world.

Travolta shines as Tony Manero in ways not evident in his similar roles as Billy Nolan, everyone's dreamboat, in *Carrie* (1976), and as the leather-jacketed Danny in *Grease* (1978), Robert Stigwood's box-office bonanza based on the Broadway musical by Jim Jacobs and Warren Casey. For all the financial success of *Grease,* due in large part to the inspired camerawork of Bill Butler, the inventive production design by Phil Jeffries, and the irresistible music, Travolta is still playing a high-school hero, a stereotyped Sha Na Na greaser. Young audiences could not get enough of Travolta, the transplanted television idol, however, and *Grease* became another superhit largely because people came to see it again and again.

Older audiences could not get enough of Paul Newman and Robert Redford, whose charming Sixties western *Butch Cassidy and the Sundance Kid* (1969) began a seemingly endless spate of "buddy" movies, including the existential angst of Al Pacino and Gene Hackman in the underrated *Scarecrow* (1973) and Paul Newman and Lee Marvin in *Pocket Money* (1972), a poorly distributed, virtually unexhibited feature scripted by Terrence Malick and based on the novel *Jim Kane* by J.P.S. Brown; the sports antics and tangled emotions of Robert De Niro and Michael Moriarty in *Bang the Drum Slowly* (1973) and George Segal and Elliott Gould in *California Split* (1974); the hijinks of black partners like Sidney Poitier and Harry Belafonte in *Buck and the Preacher* (1971); and the bizarre detective adventures of *Freebie and the Bean* (1974) with Alan Arkin and James

Karen Lynn Garney and John Travolta in John Badham's SATURDAY NIGHT FEVER (1977).

Caan. For quite a while, it seemed there were no roles for women in American film, and many Sunday feature pages tried to explain this notable lack. The money that kept raining in from the saga of Butch and Sundance also generated television movies based on subsidiary characters like Etta Place and inspired a "prequel," *Butch and Sundance: The Early Years* (1979), featuring William Katt and Tom Berenger as the neophyte gunmen.

Paul Newman and Robert Redford themselves teamed up again in another "buddy" film, the "best film" of 1973, George Roy Hill's commercial giant, *The Sting*, a testament to the value of blue eyes and bright smiles. *The Sting,* a delightful romp based on an original screenplay by David S. Ward, features the mesmerizing piano rags of Scott Joplin as interpreted and arranged by the lavishly honored Marvin Hamlisch, who also did the music for *The Way We Were* (1973), a Barbra Streisand vehicle, and the Broadway smash, *A Chorus Line*. Set in Al Capone's Chicago as ravishingly recreated by the camera of Robert Surtees, *The Sting* suffers slightly from a convoluted plot containing several narrative ruses which just do not bear scrutiny, but George Roy Hill shuffles his cards so carefully that viewers never notice the loaded deck; Hill keeps everyone busy with the mechanics of the scam and caught up in the syncopated rhythms of the polished performances by minor characters like Tom Spratley as the bogus English gentleman, Harold Gould as Kid Twist, Eileen Brennan as Billie, and Dimitra Arliss as Loretta, a much put-upon waitress. *The Sting* made the Depression look like fun, and since everything works out in a typical happy ending, audiences left the theater boogieing to Scott Joplin's catchy melodies.

Many people left the theater early to escape the terrors and incredible special effects of 1973s big film, *The Exorcist,* William Friedkin's excursion into demonology and side-show horrors. Friedkin had been depressed by the failures of both *The Birthday Party* (1968) and *The Boys in the Band* (1970) and told interviewers his new formula for success, a condescending approach to a mass audience: "I know how to do it: how to, for an hour and a half, just constantly throw everything I have at an audience and give them a real thrill. That's what they want. They don't want to go into a theater and treat it like a book. They don't even *read* books!" *The Exorcist* is a textbook case of throwing things at an audience about every five minutes or so.

40

Robert Shaw, Paul Newman, and Robert Redford in George Roy Hill's THE STING (1973).

Max Von Sydow in William Friedkin's THE EXORCIST (1973).

There is a little exposition, some philosophy and theology, a quiet interlude, and then pandemonium reigns: rooms shake, heads turn full circle on bodies, wounds fester, vomit spews forth in bilious clouds besmirching a saintly priest, a possessed adolescent girl masturbates bloodily with a crucifix as she barks blasphemies and obscenities, and hoary demons freeze the soul. America had a love-hate affair with *The Exorcist;* no one could bear to look, but everyone had to see it again and again. New York theaters were so jammed they scheduled round-the-clock screenings, and newspapers were jammed with weird tales of demonic possessions and miraculous cures. *The Exorcist* served the same role Leslie Fiedler ascribes to monstrosities in his study of *Freaks:* the film became an outlet for suppressed fantasies about sexuality, doctors, demons, and clerics, a lightning rod for our stormiest fears.

When talented director John Boorman tried to rationalize and philosophize about Pazuzu the demon in *Exorcist II—The Heretic* (1977), he chose Richard Burton as an anguished Father Lamont and Louise Fletcher as analyst Dr. Gene Tuskin, the protagonists in a global tale of the attempt to salvage the extraordinary powers of Regan (Linda Blair) and to facilitate the arrival of a Teilhard de Chardin-like evolutionary transformation of man. Unfortunately, despite some stunning visual effects, extraordinary location shooting, and fine camerawork by William A. Fraker, *Exorcist II—The Heretic* proved to be one of the least-successful sequels ever made.

Huge box-office successes like *Star Wars, Jaws, The Godfather,* and *The Exorcist* were not the only films to generate sequels or whole series in the Seventies. Hollywood producers, who overlooked the rights to Ian Fleming's James Bond novels, learned a great deal from expatriate Americans Harry Saltzman and Albert Broccoli, who turned Bond into a major business. Eleven Bond features, spanning two decades, sold over 500 million dollars worth of tickets in the United States, and another billion worldwide, and Broccoli (buying out Saltzman) planned even more Bond features, for, as he told *New York Times* interviewer Tony Chiu, "We entertain a certain audience the same as a symphony entertains a certain audience and the same as these rock groups entertain the kids." Sequels, producers assumed, had a ready-made audience, were presold, and needed less publicity; the first version served as a promotional campaign for the second, as the Empire struck back, Rocky got another title shot, or Superman met a new villain.

An example of this predilection for sequels is the *Airport* series. It began in 1970, with *Airport,* a *Grand Hotel* in the sky, featuring celebrities like Dean Martin, Helen Hayes, and Jean Seberg; every few years or so some more show-biz types would crowd on a plane that would threaten to crash, collide with another, meet' with terrorists, or otherwise be subjected to the perils of Pauline. Meanwhile inside, passengers like Helen Reddy, Gloria Swanson, and Myrna Loy would sing, swoon, and scream for two intense hours of emotionally charged self-discovery. As the decade progressed, the planes got larger and faster culminating in *Airport '80 The Concorde* (1979), featuring Alain Delon, Susan Blakely, and Bibi Andersson, but actually starring the sleek, ultramodern aircraft. In each outing, the plots in this series grew more and more ludicrous.

Serious challenges to the ingenuity of Seventies screenwriters were also posed by the continuing *Planet of the Apes* series, an almost surefire formula of costumes and ironic reversals, whether the audience was *Beneath the Planet of the Apes* (1970) or involved in the *Battle for the Planet of the Apes* (1973), the *Conquest of the Planet of the Apes* (1972), or an *Escape from the Planet of the Apes* (1971). Most producers settled, however, for two or three films based on the same material. The crypto-fascist heroics, for example, of Buford Pusser, a legendary Tennessee sheriff, were transmuted into a Bing Crosby Production glorifying a simple man who could transcend complex judicial questions and involved court procedures to assure that baddies took a terrible beating. *Walking Tall* (1973) starred Joe Don Baker as the former wrestler turned inspired gangbuster. *Walking Tall, Part 2* (1975) returned to McNairy County, but Bo Svenson played Buford; audiences did not seem to mind the switch, for the new installments still had plenty of sadism and savagery, innocents to be hurt, prostitutes to be tortured, and heads to be cracked. *The Final Chapter — Walking Tall* (1977) also starred Bo Svenson, but its popularity was eroded by unsavory stories about Pusser circulating in the national press; his big stick appeared to have some knotholes in it.

Clint Eastwood created a similar trilogy of vigilantism, viciousness, and violence in *Dirty Harry* (1971), *Magnum Force* (1973), and *The Enforcer* (1976). Dirty Harry Callahan's enemies make virtually any-

Helen Hayes in hysterics in George Seaton's AIRPORT (1970).

Charlton Heston runs for his life in Franklin Schaffner's THE PLANET OF THE APES (1967), the progenitor of many sequels.

*Joe Don Baker and Elizabeth Hartman in Phil Karlson's WALKING
TALL (1973).*

Clint Eastwood, the last gladiator, in Don Siegel's DIRTY HARRY (1971).

thing he does seem acceptable; the villains in these films include perverts, child molesters, terrorists, and uglies who enjoy dismembering young women. In this bleak universe, Harry, hampered by black, female, and inexperienced partners, liberal mayors, and media-conscious district attorneys, still manages to be the dirtiest of the dirty, even if he has to throw away his badge occasionally or turn in overzealous colleagues. His big gun manages to silence critics and criminals alike.

Even sensitive would-be folk heroes like Billy Jack (Tom Laughlin) could never be dismissed in one film. A mystic Indian creed of healthy living, ecological awareness, and martial arts proficiency highlight *Billy Jack* (1971), a film distinguished by an outstanding performance by Delores Taylor as an idealistic pacifist dealing with the anger a rape victim feels. Billy Jack is no pacifist, and his reaction to the rape sets the stage for *The Trial of Billy Jack* (1974).

No project in the Seventies was immune to sequel fever. The unlikeliest endeavors all proved worthy of repetition. *Deep Throat* (1972), for example, the *Ben-Hur* of hard-core pornography, was followed by *Deep Throat 2* (1974), a considerably softer version, still spicy enough to titillate, but aimed at a wider, more sheltered audience. The rats from *Willard* (1971) were resurrected in *Ben* (1972), just as the murderous infants of *It's Alive* (1977) came back in *It Lives Again* (1978). The daring nudists of *Harrad Experiment* (1973) continued to shed clothes and inhibitions in *Harrad Summer* (1974); *Westworld* (1973) yielded to *Futureworld* (1976); one *French Connection* (1971) led to another, *French Connection 2* (1975); and even the outrageously camp *Mandingo* (1975) was bested by the even steamier theatrics, whippings, beatings, and miscegenation of *Drum* (1977). The *Summer of '42* (1971) resulted in *The Class of '44* (1973), and the saccharine sentimentality of Erich Segal's tale of "a twenty-five-year-old girl who died," *Love Story* (1970), demanded equal time for tears in *Oliver's Story* (1978). The teen-agers who went across the *Macon County Line* (1973) had to *Return to Macon County* (1975), just as Dinah Hunter (Yvette Mimieux), who was brutalized, raped, and then escaped the *Jackson County Jail* (1976) had to return in *Outside Chance* (1978), the first nonunion film made for television, and relive her experience in an alternate version. In the Seventies, even *The Other Side of the Mountain* (1977) had its own two parts.

Tom Laughlin and Delores Taylor in BILLY JACK (1971).

When producers did not have original material of their own to justify a sequel, they frequently turned to old movie classics for material. As a result, the Seventies witnessed some of the looniest remakes conceivable. Producer Ross Hunter, for example, tried a musical version of *Lost Horizon* (1973), starring Peter Finch, Liv Ullmann, Sally Kellerman, and John Gielgud, that will never play again outside of Shangri-La. Dino De Laurentiis invested twenty-two million dollars in Jan Troell's *The Hurricane* (1979), a revamped version of John Ford's 1937 epic, which was greeted by howls of laughter. Lorenzo Semple, Jr.'s, script, set in Pago Pago circa 1920, contains some of the best unintentionally funny lines of the decade, including Trevor Howard's advice in the role of Father Malone that: "In the tropics, take passion in small doses and always with a grain of salt." The lovers in *Hurricane*, Mia Farrow and newcomer Dayton Ka'ne, obviously needed some salt tablets.

Dino De Laurentiis's other big remake, *King Kong* (1976), starring Jessica Lange as Dwan and Jeff Bridges as Jack Prescott, makes better use of the tropics, but still leaves one longing for the Merian C. Cooper–Ernest Schoedsack original. The new Kong is a complex, forty-foot-tall mechanism, weighing over six tons and capable of stepping fifteen feet in a single stride, yet the screenplay by Lorenzo Semple, Jr., is played for laughs, not thrills: Jessica Lange, for example, plays a bolder, more liberated woman who rather enjoys being blown dry after her bath by the playful Kong, and the villains, the shady magnates of Petrox Oil Company, suit an energy and ecology conscious age. In this *King Kong*, the creature has the World Trade Center to scale, where over thirty thousand unpaid extras gathered to watch his tragic death.

This huge turnout at the World Trade Plaza resulted in the largest crowd scene ever filmed and one of the most dramatic publicity stunts ever, yet director John Guillermin had no control that night over the throng, and he was forced to film as quickly as possible before the inchoate masses engulfed him, his stars, and the fallen Kong. As it was, pieces of Kong were carried home as souvenirs, and literary critic X. J. Kennedy need not have asked that night, "Who Killed King Kong?"

Many intelligent observers of the Hollywood scene express genuine alarm that the new Seventies orientation to massive profits, greater

Jessica Lange and Jeff Bridges in John Guillermin's KING KONG (1976).

and greater thrills, and more and more series, sequels, and remakes similarly threatens to cannibalize the art of cinema and dampen innovation. Louis Malle summarized these fears while working on his offbeat, New Orleans-based project, *Pretty Baby* (1978): "What worries me is that the American film industry is totally mass-oriented. . . . The trend now is to consider that if you don't have a blockbuster, you're nothing. In any industry, if your product brings in a twenty or thirty percent profit, everybody is absolutely delighted. But in the movie industry if you don't bring in three hundred percent, then you've done nothing." The result of this commitment to overkill, director Malle indicates, is that "it looks like five pictures every year are going to hit the jackpot and the rest will be considered flops." As producers tried to weed out flops before they were made and distributors tried not to release films with modest prospects, the axiom "higher and higher" in the Seventies often had as its corollary fewer and fewer.

3. When I Paint My Masterpiece

They said they were fed up with the stinking Hollywood rat race and someday they'd tell the studios to go fuck themselves and then they were going to make their own small personal pictures—pictures about real human beings, pictures with heart. That's what it's all about, they said.
ELEANOR PERRY, *Blue Pages*

WHILE HOLLYWOOD in the late Sixties was hardly the capital of the decadence that avant-garde filmmaker Kenneth Anger immortalized in his long-suppressed underground classic turned best-selling coffee table showpiece, *Hollywood Babylon* (Straight Arrow Books, 1975), the film industry was being pressured to change the Production Code it originally adopted in 1930. The code expressly forbade a seal of compliance to films which featured "excessive and lustful kissing," "sex perversion or any inference of it," "miscegenation," "obscenity in word, gesture, reference, song, joke," or "complete nudity," and demanded that "the treatment of bedrooms be governed by good taste and delicacy." For years this had meant coy use of sheets, separate beds even for married couples, and passionate embraces that faded to long shots of flames licking at logs in fireplaces, thunderstorms with phallic bolts of lightning, long trains entering dark tunnels, and restless surf pounding rhythmically against rocky coasts. Such sly sexual metaphors did not fit the swinging Sixties or the let-it-all-hang-out mood of the early Seventies. In an era of massage parlors and nude encounter groups, audiences were curious, yellow and blue, and craved greater realism. Antonioni's *Blow Up* (1966) with its nude nymphets was distributed without a code seal by an MGM American subsidiary, while the code managed to stretch enough to allow nudity in *The Pawnbroker* (1965), adult language in *Who's Afraid of Virginia Woolf?* (1966), and slow-motion violence in *Bonnie and Clyde* (1967).

In November 1968, however, the Production Code gave way to a new Code and Rating Administration, which eventually changed its name to the Classification and Rating Administration. Films were no longer subject to prior restraint, nor were they all to be seen as aimed at the same audience. After a few modifications in the lettering, four distinct groupings were institutionalized: G for general audiences, PG for fare which required some parental discretion about the suitability of some material contained therein for pre-teen-age children, R which demanded a responsible adult accompany any viewer under seventeen, and X—films suitable for adults. In the first ten years of the classification system, according to a tally published in *Variety* (November 1, 1978), 4,590 films were evaluated, with 793 (17%) receiving a G rating, 1,721 (37%) a PG, 1,818 (40%) an R, and 258 (6%) an X. When one excludes independent productions from this tally, the so-called major and minor companies (Allied Artists, American International, Avco Embassy, Buena Vista, Cinerama, Columbia, MGM, National General, Paramount, Twentieth Century-Fox, United Artists, Universal, and Warner Brothers) were responsible for 2,086 films, 45% of the total rated, and their features received 474 (23%) G ratings, 975 (47%) PG, 598 (29%) R, and 39 (2%) X. Mainstream Hollywood was clearly becoming a PG town, where parental discretion abounded, and many deals included a specification that the resultant film be planned, and if necessary recut, to meet the unwritten criteria for this rating: maturity without too much nudity, action without too much gore, and bold dialogue with most expletives deleted.

The new classification did not solve all the problems Hollywood faced with censorship and the courts. America was in turmoil over changing sexual mores, and that confusion was reflected in the Supreme Court's June 1973 ruling that the determination of whether a work of art was obscene or not depended on the standards of the local community. Sexually liberated Esalen obviously was not the same as Evansville, and it was a long way from the Bible Belt to a topless bar, as George C. Scott discovered in Paul Schrader's *Hardcore* (1979). The same decade that witnessed a Presidential Commission on Pornography offer some very enlightened and permissive recommendations also saw the Georgia Supreme Court uphold the conviction on obscenity charges of a theater operator who dared to screen the cerebral, R-rated *Carnal Knowledge* (1971), a prestigious project directed by Mike Nichols and starring Art Garfunkel and Jack Nicholson.

While Hollywood and the courts fumed and fussed about bare pudenda, bloody bullet holes, and filthy language, a whole new industry sprang up, with self-proclaimed "triple X" ratings, flooding the market with "hard core" footage. The so-called "soft core" pornography of the Seventies usually included total nudity, simulated sex, and raunchy dialogue, while "hard core" meant detailed close-ups of the genitalia, so-called "beaver" and "split beaver" shots, and authentic sex acts, with erection, penetration, and ejaculation carefully, though frequently clumsily, documented. The doyen of celebrity watchers, Earl Wilson, was so "enraged" by "the peddlers of obscenity" that he wrote the well-illustrated, lavishly detailed, and provocatively titled *Show Business Laid Bare* (1974) to describe in fevered prose the lewd and lurid horrors he had seen and that he felt his readers should condemn and avoid. Around the same time, his son brought *Let My People Come,* a nude revue which made *Oh! Calcutta* look tame, to a Greenwich Village nightspot. Still another New York writer, Janet Maslin, was so shocked by the violence in George A. Romero's unrated *Dawn of the Dead* (1979) that she wrote what must be the most infamous film review ever published in the *New York Times*, condemning the film though she admitted she "was able to sit through only the first 15 minutes."

The 1968 classification system could not please everyone. Independents went to court to prove the majors were getting preferential treatment, while other special-interest groups complained there were too many Polish jokes, too many animals being hurt, too many unflattering pictures of chiropracters, doctors, and lawyers, and too many Italians cast as gangsters. Psychologists denounced the omnipresence of violence, and major church groups scored nihilism, nudity, and blasphemy. Studios argued that an R rating excluded adolescents from films designed for them (*Woodstock,* 1970; and *Gimme Shelter,* 1970) and sometimes appealed on artistic grounds to have classifications changed (*All the President's Men,* 1976). Newspapers often refused advertisements for X-rated films, even when the material was quite serious adult fare like Stanley Kubrick's chilling masterpiece, *A Clockwork Orange* (1971). Sometimes, two different versions of the

55

Jack Nicholson and Art Garfunkel in Mike Nichols' CARNAL KNOWLEDGE (1971).

same film would be distributed: *Saturday Night Fever* (1977), originally R-rated, was later rereleased in a PG version to ensure, the studio blurbs declared, that everyone had a chance to enjoy the magnetism of John Travolta cavorting to the music of the Bee Gees.

For all this jumble of opinion and reaction, one major fact should not be obscured. The 1968 revisions did achieve their self-proclaimed objectives: "to encourage artistic expression by expanding creative freedom" and "to assure that the freedom which encourages the artist remains responsible and sensitive to the standards of the larger society." The classification system has allowed Hollywood in the Seventies considerably expanded freedom of expression, while it provides the means by which concerned adults can make informed decisions about the films they wish to see. Even a casual consideration of some of the major films of the Seventies suggests how much the industry has changed: it is hard to imagine *Coming Home* (1978) for example, without the adultery, explicit sexuality, and antiwar rhetoric; or *Carrie* (1976) without its opening menstruation sequences in the girls' locker room; or *Dog Day Afternoon* (1975) without its homosexual motif. Without the new classification system, there might never have been a domestic release of *Last Tango in Paris* (1972). In fact, without the institutionalized recognition that not every film need be suitable for every viewer, the new Hollywood could never have been born; it would not have attracted film makers of great vision and insight nor could it have reflected the realities of life in the America of Watergate and Vietnam, an America discovering its own hell just the other side of "The Gates of Eden."

The Grand Prize winner at the Cannes Film Festival in 1970, *M*A*S*H*, exemplifies many of the changes the new classification system permitted; rated R, *M*A*S*H* is a foul-mouthed, raucous, anti-establishment comedy, combining gallows humor, sexual slapstick, and outrageous satire. Its surgeon heroes, Hawkeye (Donald Sutherland) and Trapper John (Elliott Gould), are sensitive buddies warring relentlessly against authority, hypocrisy, pomp, and circumstance. In the operating room, their cool competence coexists with a lively banter as smutty as it is hilarious; on the golf course and football field, they display a studied nonchalance equaled only by their guile. These two Don Juans manage to combine a mission of mercy with a spree at a whorehouse, and only the brass end up with

The establishment as villain in George Romero's THE CRAZIES (1973).

Sissy Spacek in Brian DePalma's CARRIE (1976).

egg on their face. Absolutely nothing is sacred in *M*A*S*H:* Fred Williamson, for example, plays a character named Spearchucker, Rene Auberjonois is Dago Red, and Jo Ann Pflug is Lt. Dish. Major "Hot Lips" Houlihan, played by Sally Kellerman, not only sleeps with the ineffectual Major Frank Burns (Robert Duvall) but finds herself naked in front of an attentive audience when the boys collapse the shower tent to see who wins a big bet on the "natural" color of her hair. When the well-endowed dentist, Painless Pole (John Schuck), worries about his impotency, the crew stages a mock "Last Supper" for this phallic saint and then assures a proper resurrection.

M*A*S*H was written by Ring Lardner, Jr., one of the Hollywood Ten, and based on the novel by Richard Hooker, a doctor stationed at a Mobile Army Surgical Hospital during the Korean War. As producer Ingo Preminger noted, "No one sees the war the way the surgeons do." The man who brought this unique vision to American audiences, combined it with the irreverence of his fifteen-year-old son's theme music "Suicide is Painless," and added his own personal brand of sanity and sensitivity was Robert Altman, a well-paid television director who had made several small films in the Sixties but who was destined to emerge as the most influential filmmaker of the Seventies, a genius as prolific as he was inspired.

Robert Altman's next film, *Brewster McCloud,* released in December 1970, proved an unwelcome Christmas present for the mass audience, yet this convoluted disquisition on the entwined fates of men and birds with its sly commentary on dreams, innocence, and the artificial universe of the Houston Astrodome has proven a favorite in retrospectives of the director's career. *Brewster McCloud* drowns the detective-chase genre in a flood of bird droppings and disrupts the off-key, out-of-step patriotism of sports rituals as it tears the wings off all the fairy godmother stories ever written. Like many of Altman's most obscure works, it constantly weighs knowledge against intuition and experience, reality against illusion, the everyday against the mythic, and the physical and tangible against the psychological and ethereal. Brewster, played by Bud Cort, cannot sustain his free flight under the dome without the tutelage of Sally Kellerman as Louise, yet her ministrations demand that he reject the blandishments of the wide-eyed Suzanne, a Leonard Cohen vision played by Shelley Duvall, and the bountiful Hope, played by Jennifer Salt.

60

Sally Kellerman in Robert Altman's M*A*S*H (1970).

Warren Beatty as John McCabe, the hero of Altman's 1972 Western, *McCabe and Mrs. Miller,* another damaged archangel convinced he has "poetry" within, fears that Constance Miller (Julie Christie), his opium-addicted partner in a mining-town bordello, will "freeze" his soul. For this dreamy daguerrotype of fire and ice, Altman spent almost his entire budget on sets by Leon Ericksen and then instructed cinematographer Vilmos Zsigmond to use yellow filters; for background music, Canadian poet Leonard Cohen weaves melancholy images of his beautiful losers. Altman's next project, *Images* (1972), shot in Canada with photography by Vilmos Zsigmond and music by John Williams, one of Altman's earliest "women's pictures," afforded Susannah York her most challenging role since *The Killing of Sister George* (1969). The claustrophobia of the sets, however, the jarring shifts in point of view, and the overly literary conception made the narrative heavy going. *The Long Goodbye* (1973), based on the well-known Raymond Chandler story, returned to the more linear world of genre films, where Altman set a modernized Marlowe adrift in a psychedelic Los Angeles, crowded with bare-breasted young nature freaks, garish neon supermarkets, wealthy suicidal Hemingwayesque artists, and Mexican double-crosses. Detective story buffs were enraged at his "distortions," but Altman used Leigh Brackett's screenplay, John Williams' music, Vilmos Zsigmond's camerawork, and Elliott Gould's spacey performance opposite celebrity Nina van Pallandt to forge another effective vision of a stunted hero confronting an almost incomprehensible universe.

In 1974, Altman offered his "Romeo and Juliet," *Thieves Like Us,* a remake of *They Live By Night,* set in Depression-racked America and haunted by the eerie cadences of populist Father Coughlin. Bowie (Keith Carradine) and Keechie (Shelley Duvall), an emaciated Bonnie and Clyde seemingly modeled on Walker Evans photographs, are more suited to quiet romancing on a sunny afternoon than desperate escapes and bold shoot-outs; these Coca Cola-sipping criminals are more victims than predators. *California Split* (1974) features still another set of drifters, Bill Denny (George Segal) and Charlie Walters (Elliott Gould), looking for a big score at the gaming tables. Altman's father, a wealthy insurance broker, was a compulsive gambler, and his son has the milieu down pat, including the cornflakes with warm beer breakfasts. Even when the two stumblebums finally do hit the jackpot, Bill tries desperately to split the real wisdom with his friend: "Charlie, it don't mean a fucking thing."

In *Nashville* (1975), Altman's most popular film, a kaleidoscopic two and a half hours full of adulteries, betrayals, epiphanies, disillusionments, and assassination, all set in the capital of country music, this theme is reiterated in the haunting lyric, "It don't worry me." Altman seems similarly sanguine about his complex plot, two dozen feature players, and diverse musical interludes. Much of *Nashville* was improvised, with the stars preparing their own songs, yet few productions have ever demonstrated a more fluid directorial style.

Altman's subsequent film, *Buffalo Bill and the Indians, or Sitting Bull's History Lesson* (1976) a commercial failure despite its bankable star, Paul Newman, and its critically acclaimed source, Arthur Kopit's *Indians,* focused on the "star," his producer (Joel Grey), and his publicist (Kevin McCarthy), presenting a Buffalo Bill who was truly defunct, caught up by his own mythology, preoccupied by showmanship, and mesmerized by his reflection in a mirror.

Three Women (1977), another enigmatic dream opus, presents three incomplete personalities in need of greater fullness and coherent images: Millie Lammoreaux (Shelley Duvall), a rambling monologist, cannot see beyond her *Redbook* world of cheese in tubes, endless futile dates, backless dresses, and a weary job in a geriatric center, while her adoring roommate Pinky Rose (Sissy Spacek) struggles through a suicide attempt, and Willie Hart (Janice Rule) draws giant murals of reptilian creatures.

Women also reign in Altman's 1978 feature, *A Wedding.* Like *Nashville, A Wedding* weaves vignettes involving over forty characters into a mordant satire of wealth, class, and the American family. Two families have plenty to hide, but *A Wedding* uncovers all their strategies to "be free" as Leonard Cohen's "Bird on a Wire." After *A Wedding,* Altman turned unsuccessfully to science fiction as a vehicle for social comment in *Quintet,* his grim fairy tale starring Paul Newman, set amidst the icy ruins of a nuclear war, where the old destructive, competitive gaming impulses are destroying players and leaving terrible carnage as the Dark Ages closes in on heroes.

Altman's last film in the Seventies returns to his comic mode. *A Perfect Couple,* a gentle rock music opus featuring the group "Keepin' 'Em Off the Streets," mocks computer dating as it limns a

Sissy Spacek and Shelley Duvall in Robert Altman's THREE WOMEN (1977).

moving portrait of human needs and foibles. Its improbably star-crossed lovers are Alex Theodopoulus (Paul Dooley), the scion of a Greek clan given to classical music, Oedipal conflicts, and sinister repression; and Sheila Shea (Marta Heflin), a loner in a commune given to soft rock, open marriage, and bisexuality. These opposites do not attract; they collide, career, separate, then find each other.

In addition to the thirteen films he directed, Robert Altman, through his Lion's Gate Films, also left his mark on the decade by encouraging young filmmakers and daring projects, including Alan Rudolph's symphony of ''the city of one night stands,'' the underrated *Welcome to L.A.* (1977); his tone poem *Remember My Name* (1978), an elegiac character study starring Geraldine Chaplin and showcasing the gutsy blues of Alberta Hunter; Robert Benton's *The Late Show* (1977), a zany thriller pairing two unlikely sleuths, Art Carney and Lily Tomlin; and Robert Young's *Rich Kids* (1979), a *Bildungsroman* where the children's sanity discomfits their neurotic parents.

Contrasted to Altman's sprawling canon, Terrence Malick's two outings as director, *Badlands* (1974) and *Days of Heaven* (1979), make this Harvard-educated Rhodes scholar-philosopher seem positively laconic. *Badlands,* loosely based on Charles Starkweather's killing spree, depends heavily for its effect on the rambling musings of the unrepentant Holly (Sissy Spacek), a media-obsessed ingenue with all the style of *True Confessions* magazine. Holly's innocence is at once laughable and frightening: her daredevil adventures with her garbage-man James Dean, Kit (Martin Sheen), ''the most trigger-happy person'' she ever met, are narrated with a juvenile sentimentality that ignores the enormity of the crimes committed. Holly finds more mystery in the death of her pet fish than in all the killings that follow; she is an American girl looking for life and love the way it is in movies and magazines, the way ''it is supposed to be.''

Malick emphasizes the tension between dream and fact, media event and actuality with poetic visuals of the plains of South Dakota and Montana and a studied musical commentary. Nat King Cole's rendition of ''A Blossom Fell'' moves Kit and Holly to stop and dance, but as they attempt to escape America, the subtle and involved melodies of French composer Erik Satie propel them. For the dramatic burning of Holly's house and the capture of Kit, Holly's symbolic loss of father and lover, Malick uses the choral works of Carl Orff.

Robert Altman directing Carol Burnett in A WEDDING (1978).

Sissy Spacek in Terrence Malick's BADLANDS (1974).

Lee Marvin and Sissy Spacek in Michael Ritchie's PRIME CUT (1970).

Similar artistic choices make Malick's Dreiser-like narrative of *belle époque* America, *Days of Heaven*, a radiant delight. Filmed in Canada by New Wave cinematographer Nestor Almendros, who conscientiously imitates the look of Vermeer, this almost biblical parable of a husband (Richard Gere) and wife (Brooke Adams) posing as brother and sister who deceive and murder a rich farmer (Sam Shepard), also profits from the double-edged narration of the unsophisticated kid sister (Linda Manz). She often unwittingly captures the chivalry and romance in this Cinderella story gone sour; recalling the good times, she philosophizes that "We were all living like kings, just nothing to do all day but lie around cracking jokes. . . . I'm telling you, the rich got it all figured out." Malick's poor protagonists never quite figure it out or succeed as royalty; law and order imprisons their laughter and dreams.

Director Michael Ritchie, a Harvard-educated historian, also treats would-be heroes caught up by contemporary institutions in his Preston Sturges-like comedies. Unlike documentary maker Frederick Wiseman, who allows his editing to reveal his attitudes in *High School* (1969), *Law and Order* (1970), *Hospital* (1971), *Juvenile Court* (1974), *Welfare* (1975), and *Meat* (1977), Ritchie depends on literate scripts, stellar acting, and bitter irony. In *Downhill Racer* (1969), Robert Redford, as skier David Chappellet, learns the world is just full of ex-champions; in *The Candidate* (1972), Redford as the issue-oriented Bill McKay discovers why politicians do not know what to do next. Ritchie's most macabre and poorly understood work, *Prime Cut* (1970), shows that even tough gangsters can end up as sausages. In one of the blackest comic exchanges ever, the hoods actually debate what to do with this processed corpse: "What should I do with them?" "Did you know Murphy?" "Yeah." "Was he a good guy?" "Yeah." "Well, bury him." The young contestants in *Smile* (1975) are so much meat on the hoof in Ritchie's acid portrait of Santa Rosa's "Young American Miss" pageant. "Big Bob" Freelander (Bruce Dern), car salesman and contest director in *Smile,* professes a Nixonian faith in progress, even as his heir snaps Polaroid nudes for classmates. Only Andy DiCarlo (Nicholas Pavor), an impotent Dagwood Bumstead, understands the real humiliations of his "Exhausted Rooster Ceremony," the Bears' own perverse pageant.

The Bad News Bears (1976) turns alcoholic has-been Morris Buttermaker (Walter Matthau) loose in the pressure-cooker world of little league baseball, a territory so larded with sentimentality that much of Ritchie's message slipped by audiences. America, in fact demanded the return of the underdogs in *The Bad News Bears in Breaking Training* (1977), directed by Michael Pressman and featuring a fine performance by young actor Jimmy Baio as Carmen Ronzonni, and *The Bad News Bears Go to Japan* (1978), a less-successful venture, produced by Michael Ritchie but directed by John Berry.

Professional football provided the backdrop for Ritchie's *Semi-Tough* (1977), a wild and woolly lampoon of contemporary fads, including the EST-like Bismark Energy Attack Training, Movagenics, which suggests one crawl one's way to contentment, and Pelfing, a torturous massage advocated by Carla Pelf (Lotte Lenya). *An Almost Perfect Affair* (1979) delineates the cinema-as-art, film-as-business dichotomy so evident in the competition for fame and love at the Cannes Film Festival.

Paul Mazursky's risqué blockbuster *Bob and Carol and Ted and Alice* (1969) gave him the power in Hollywood to make small films when packagers demanded pictures that cost more. *Alex in Wonderland* (1970), a Fellini-like fantasy about a movie director (Donald Sutherland) seeking inspiration à la *8½* in the New Hollywood, and *Blume in Love* (1973), a contemporary romance replete with an improbable reconciliation in Venice and a joyous pregnancy, both failed commercially, but the success of *Harry and Tonto* (1974), including an Oscar for lead Art Carney, kept Mazursky in wonderland. *Harry and Tonto,* a geriatric *Easy Rider,* chronicles the odyssey of Harry Combes, a seventy-two-year-old widowed, retired teacher forced by circumstances to become a pilgrim in America with only his cat Tonto as companion. "If life is a river," Harry speculates, "a man has to struggle or he'll drown." So, despite all the confusion in America, the fortress mentality in his son's suburban New Jersey home, the senility of his Midwest sweetheart, the psychologically ravaged singles in Western condominiums, noble Indians in jail, and hitchhiking prostitutes, Harry's hegira goes on. As Harry tells Tonto, "Life is confusing, but I'm doing my best to get on with it."

Talented young comedian Jimmy Baio as Carmen Ronzonni in Michael Pressman's THE BAD NEWS BEARS IN BREAKING TRAINING *(1977).*

Art Carney in Paul Mazursky's HARRY AND TONTO (1974).

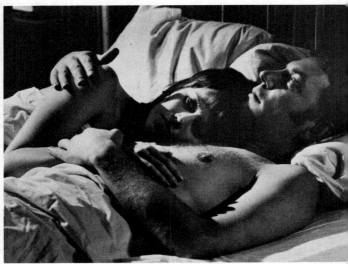

Jane Fonda and Donald Sutherland in Alan Pakula's KLUTE (1971).

Confusion challenges the young artists in Mazursky's autobiographical *Next Stop Greenwich Village* (1976), as this Brooklyn College graduate lovingly recreates the excitement of first love, first dope, and first failure, amid the coffee shops and lofts of Bleecker Street. *An Unmarried Woman* (1978), another love song to the Big Apple, vibrates with the energy of the new village, Soho, where one of the new women of the Seventies, Erica, played by Jill Clayburgh, discovers her personal worth and real independence, long smothered in her earlier upper East Side marriage. *Phil and Willie* (1980) combines all Mazursky's themes—New York, young love, and the quest for personal identity—in an affectionate comedy about Willie Kaufman (Michael Ontkean), a high-school English teacher who would rather be a jazz pianist; Phil D'Amica (Ray Sharkey), a photographer who would like to be an intellectual; and a Kentuckian who would like to be an urbanite (Margot Kidder), a threesome who form Mazursky's Seventies homage to Truffaut's *Jules and Jim.*

Alan Pakula's *Klute* (1971) pays homage to audience expectations with its terrifying shots of a prostitute stalked by a sadistic killer, but its unusual treatment of Bree Daniels' quiet moments alone revealed Jane Fonda's enormous improvisational talents and the director's mastery of mood. Pakula falters somewhat in *Love and Pain and the Whole Damn Thing* (1973), though the pairing of Maggie Smith and Timothy Bottoms might have stymied even Pakula's mentor, Robert Mulligan, the director of seven features Pakula produced before making *Klute*. *The Parallax View* (1974) is Pakula at his best, enmeshing journalist Frady (Warren Beatty) in a wide-reaching assassination plot, engineered by a sophisticated cabal who screen all their "lone misfit" candidates with a cinematic Rorschach test; the test sequence itself is one of the most celebrated in the film, manipulating the audience as it bombards Beatty's psyche. Pakula admits his fascination with the oblique, urging that "It is terribly important to give an audience a lot of things they may not get as well as those they will, so that finally the film does take on a texture and is not just simplistic communication." *All the President's Men* (1976) depends heavily on textures; the bright lights of the meticulously recreated *Washington Post* offices, the heavy clang of the typewriter, and the shadowy underground of "Deep Throat" carry this Watergate drama far beyond the normal conventions of journalist-as-detective adventures.

Perhaps only Pakula could have turned the complex Watergate story into pulsating entertainment for the masses. *Comes a Horseman* (1978), however, relies too heavily on textures; even Jane Fonda's extraordinary performance cannot breathe life into hackneyed material about cattle barons, poisoned legacies, and ancestral feuds. Pakula's next project, *Starting Over* (1979), based on Dan Wakefield's novel and starring Burt Reynolds, Jill Clayburgh, and Candice Bergen, revealed his sharp comic sense, his ability to coax performances from stars, and his eye for contemporary foibles.

Hal Ashby had plenty of opportunities in the Seventies to work with leading actors and writers. *The Landlord* (1970), his modest debut, featured a fine script by Bill Gunn and inspired clowning by Pearl Bailey and Diana Sands, but audiences did not seem ready for his comedy about a concerned white boy, Elgar Enders (Beau Bridges), and his travails as slumlord. *Harold and Maude* (1971), a bizarre romance between a suicidal prankster (Bud Cort) and a dotty old woman (Ruth Gordon) garnered a huge cult, enamoured of the iconoclasm and *Mad* magazine humor in the excellent script by Colin Higgins (*Silver Streak*, 1976; *Foul Play*, 1978). Robert Towne, whose *Chinatown* script won the Oscar in 1974, wrote Ashby's next two screenplays, his breakthrough film, *The Last Detail* (1973), and 1975s cause célèbre, *Shampoo*. *The Last Detail*, a showcase for Jack Nicholson's temper tantrums, concerns two veteran seamen's "chicken shit" duties on Shore Patrol escorting a naïve young sailor (Randy Quaid) accused of petty theft to the stockade. *The Last Detail* shocked audiences with its salty dialogue, but Towne defended it in a December 1975 *American Film* interview: "When Columbia said that wouldn't it be better to have twenty 'motherfuckers' instead of forty 'motherfuckers,'" I said no, because then you'd lose the point that these men can't do anything more than swear." Before the 1968 classification system, the number of "motherfuckers" could not have been an issue.

Shampoo, loosely based on the exploits of Beverly Hills hairdresser Gene Shacove, starred Warren Beatty as George, the stylist who admits he "fucks them all" without finding real satisfaction. This R-rated social satire demonstrated how free-wheeling classifications could be in a key scene at a political fund-raising dinner: Jackie (Julie Christie) purrs to George across a table, "I want to suck your cock,"

Hal Ashby directing Otis Young and Jack Nicholson in THE LAST DETAIL (1973).

Julie Christie and Warren Beatty in Hal Ashby's SHAMPOO (1975).

then ducks under the table exclaiming, "Oh God, let me suck it." Even in a film which begins with an orgasm interrupted by a phone call, this dialogue is pretty heady stuff. Warren Beatty's later explanations of his characterization in *Shampoo* might also be seen as a comment on the changes new directors were making in cinema: "There is an ambivalence in that character and his whole generation, having been told in formative years that life should be led one way, and that there were certain rules of sexuality and monogamy that had to be followed, and then having been told later in life that the rules don't apply any more." Hal Ashby's *Bound for Glory* (1976) showed a Woody Guthrie (David Carradine) too big for rules, though its major strength was Haskell Wexler's camerawork. *Coming Home* (1978) swept the best acting awards, with Ashby's principals, Jane Fonda and Jon Voight, making the most of a Waldo Salt script which strongly suggests that the old rules of patriotism and fidelity do not apply in the twisted America of stuffy officers' clubs, dilapidated veterans' hospitals, and a war characterized by atrocities like My Lai.

Unspeakable brutality is the hallmark of Sam Peckinpah, whose slow-motion close-ups of bullet holes erupting in torrents of gore and bold celebrations of the Western myth and the cult of machismo in *The Wild Bunch* (1969) unleashed a blood-red tide on American screens. Peckinpah could be sentimental, lyrical, and nostalgic in Westerns like *The Ballad of Cable Hogue* (1970) and the rodeo-based *Junior Bonner* (1972), and even funny in *Convoy* (1978), his spirited ode to tavern brawling, cross-country truckers, and citizen-band radio; but mostly Peckinpah was mean, dark, and brutal in rape-revenge fantasies like *Straw Dogs* (1971) and *Bring Me the Head of Alfredo Garcia* (1974), violent detective chases (*The Getaway,* 1972), nihilistic espionage adventures (*The Killer Elite,* 1975), and somber war dramas (*The Cross of Iron,* 1977). Peckinpah's *Pat Garrett and Billy the Kid* (1973), by far the best Western of the decade, profits handsomely from Bob Dylan's hauntingly beautiful music: a key death scene is marvelously underscored by "Knocking on Heaven's Door" and langorous shots of Western vistas. Peckinpah explores all the ambivalence in this confrontation between an aging, newly married sheriff (James Coburn) and feckless youth (Kris Kristofferson) till it is clear, as Pat tells Billy, "Us old boys shouldn't be doing this to one another."

James Coburn in Sam Peckinpah's PAT GARRETT AND BILLY THE KID (1973).

If Peckinpah brought the out-of-doors and open roads to American screens, another whole group of directors were devoted to urban projects. New York University-educated Martin Scorsese, for example, obviously felt more at home on the *Mean Streets* (1973) of Little Italy than he did filming the low-budget *Boxcar Bertha* (1972); even his *Alice Doesn't Live Here Anymore* (1974) works best when Alice settles down and takes a job in the diner. *Taxi Driver* (1976), Scorsese's *magnum opus,* with an overblown score by Bernard Herrmann (*Citizen Kane,* 1941; *North by Northwest,* 1959; *Psycho,* 1960), is primarily an essay detailing how 42nd Street porno joints, lonely dark streets glistening with rain, and the squalor of hustling on the lower East Side transform cabbie Travis Bickle (Robert De Niro) into a kamikaze commando, modeled after, screenwriter Paul Schrader acknowledges, would-be assassin Arthur Bremer and his diaries. *New York, New York* (1977) is all the title implies, a valentine to New York City in the Forties, seen just as it appeared in movies of the same era. *The Last Waltz* (1978), an indoor concert film with interviews, reestablished Scorsese as editor *par excellence,* for he had begun the decade supervising the mammoth assembly of sprawling rough footage into *Woodstock* (1970).

New York-born John Cassavetes remained true to the spirit of his underground hits *Shadows* (1961) and *Faces* (1968) throughout the Seventies, ignoring the demands of the mass audience, relying instead on his hand-held camera, prolonged close-ups, grainy textures, and lengthy improvised monologs to provide revelations. Cassavetes may have too jaundiced a perspective on a mythic "boys' night out" in *Husbands* (1970) and too exotic a variation on *Love Story* in *Minnie and Moskowitz* (1971), but his *A Woman Under the Influence* (1974) features a luminescent performance by his wife, Gena Rowlands; as Mabel Longhetti, she turns a simple-minded tract about a wife and mother driven crazy by her family and chauvinistic husband into an agonizingly meticulous portrait of the oppression of poverty, ignorance, and barbaric sexual mores. Mabel flounders in a maze of discarded beer cans, leftover spaghetti, and dirty dishes until her personality slowly crumbles in submission. The disintegration of a small-time strip-show operator in *The Killing of a Chinese Bookie* (1976) elicited an outstanding performance from Ben Gazzara as Cosmo Vitelli, a man whose dreams are crushed by debt. Cosmo demands his strippers act out pageants like "An Evening in Paris" and "The Gunfight at O.K. Corral," but his own shoot-outs with gangsters are clumsy, bloody affairs, sordid and demeaning. Unfortunately, *The Killing of a Chinese Bookie* was hampered by poor distribution, as were Cassavetes' next two projects with his wife, *Opening Night* (1977) and *One Summer Night*.

Director John G. Avildsen began his career with poorly distributed nudies like *Turn on to Love* (1967), *Guess What We Learned at School Today* (1969), and *Cry Uncle* (1971), but *Joe* (1970), based on an explosive screenplay by Norman Wexler and starring one of the decade's leading character actors, Peter Boyle (*Slither,* 1972; *The Friends of Eddie Coyle,* 1973; *Hardcore,* 1979), established him as a commercial director. Avildsen treated big issues in a riveting fashion in *Joe,* reducing the much vaunted "generation gap" of the Seventies to a chilling bloodbath. Audiences loved this simplification and melodrama; by decade's end, *Joe 2* was ready. Avildsen favors big emotions, and after the atypical *Roger the Stoolie* (1972), he put Jack Lemmon through his Oscar-winning theatrics in *Save the Tiger* (1973), another ostentatiously "searing" generation-gap soap opera. Lemmon plays Harry Stoner, a basically honest garment maker wondering what has happened to his youth, his heroes, and his country; Harry seems just as confused by changing sexual mores as he is bewildered by the collapse of his trade. When Harry schemes with gangsters to burn his plant down for insurance, they meet in a porno theater; the clothier's musings on baseball and the demise of virtue baffle his seminude, liberated, hippie paramour; and the buyer he is entertaining in hopes of a sale dies in the midst of kinky sex with two prostitutes Harry hired. Like so many Seventies film heroes, Harry Stoner is lost in a revolution profoundly psychic, social, and sexual.

Avildsen's *W. W. and the Dixie Dancekings* (1976) is an amusing but corny showcase for Burt Reynolds and Art Carney, but his *Rocky* (1976) became the most imitated feature of the decade, an all-stops-out, sentimental celebration of a million-to-one shot who just had to endure, "The Italian Stallion," Rocky Balboa (Sylvester Stallone). Newcomer Stallone staked his fortune on *Rocky* and came up a big winner; though he replaced Avildsen as director for the first sequel, *Rocky II* (1979), the writer-actor acknowledged that Avildsen had taught him the big secret of successful filmmaking: "Go slow."

Ben Gazzara starring as Cosmo Vitelli in John Cassavetes' THE KILLING OF A CHINESE BOOKIE (1976).

Strippers acting out pageants in THE KILLING OF A CHINESE BOOKIE.

Jack Lemmon in John Avildsen's SAVE THE TIGER (1973).

Avildsen took his own advice in *Slow Dancing in the Big City* (1978), the lachrymose tale of a ballerina (Anne Ditchburn) whose debut at Lincoln Center will also be her finale. Avildsen himself provided the best criticism of this film: "Of course, I realized as I was making the film that it might be called 'Rocky with Tights.' But more people are going to see it everyday."

Another urban poet with his eye on relevance and the box office, William Friedkin, found himself in the headlines twice in 1979, once when he divorced Jeanne Moreau and again when militant gays demanded he stop shooting the violent *Cruising,* a sensational story of a detective (Al Pacino) who becomes a murderer because he cannot cope with his sexuality. Friedkin's *The Boys in the Band* (1970), based on Mart Crowley's play, treated homosexuals sympathetically, but there were many rumors about a deleted sequence in the smash hit *The French Connection* (1971) that showed detective Jimmy Doyle (Gene Hackman) being systematically and pleasurably humiliated by a black prostitute into chains and leather. Hackman continued the true-life adventures of "Popeye" Doyle in *French Connection II,* a French postcard etched in dark tones by director John Franken-heimer, who should have spent more time on chase sequences. Meanwhile William Friedkin made the sock-it-to-them daddy of all demonic possession films, *The Exorcist* (1973), a model for two-word-titled thrillers like *The Omen* (1976) and *The Sentinel* (1977). Friedkin then essayed his own remake, *Sorcerer* (1977), an expensive but garbled version of Henri-Georges Clouzot's classic suspense film, *The Wages of Fear* (1953). Friedkin's next project, *The Brink's Job* (1978) could not bear the weight of its own notoriety. After the stunning, well-publicized robbery on set and a federal grand jury investigation into kickbacks to gangsters in Boston to facilitate filming, the bungling of Tony Pino (Peter Falk) and Joe McGinnis (Peter Boyle), two inept crooks who almost got away with a multimillion dollar heist, seemed small potatoes.

A good script was hard to find in the turbulent Seventies, so writers often found it easy to move from their desks to a director's chair. Paul Schrader, for example, worked with his brother Leonard to transform some source material from Sydney A. Glass into his hard-hitting directorial debut *Blue Collar* (1978), a depressing, profane study of corrupt unions, betrayed confidences, and class antagonisms in an auto plant. *Blue Collar* takes a hard Marxist line: "Everything they do, the way they pit the lifers against the new boys, the old against the young, the black against the white, is meant to keep us in our place." *Hardcore* (1978), Schrader's relatively chaste excursion into perversion, depravity, and Calvinist predestination, starred George C. Scott on a sojourn in Sodom and Gomorroh trying to save his daughter from destruction in a "snuff" film. *American Gigolo* (1979), delayed by the withdrawal of John Travolta, might not have transcendental style, but it still received substantial backing from Freddie Fields productions; the cast features the talented Richard Gere and beautiful Lauren Hutton in a convoluted mystery more notable for the male fashions on display than any sustained emotion.

Some other writers who managed to turn into superstar directors include John Milius, whose particular brew of masculinity, Americanism, and ornate symbolism resulted in *Dillinger* (1973), an unusually acute treatment of the psychic link between G-man (Ben Johnson) and his *doppelgänger* gangster (Warren Oates); *The Wind and the Lion* (1975), a popular epic with a bigger than life Teddy Roosevelt (Brian Keith) blustering through a *contretemps* with an overreaching sheik, Raisuli (Sean Connery), who kidnaps then charms the stuffy Eden Pedicaris (Candice Bergen); and *Big Wednesday* (1978), an elephantine attempt to equate surfing and the quest for the Holy Grail. Michael Crichton, Harvard-physician-turned-popular-novelist, directed *Westworld* (1973), his energetic and imaginative takeoff on grown-up Disneyland, inhabited by robots; *Coma* (1978), a topical mystery about organ transplants and unwilling donors, featuring Geneviéve Bujold as a forceful heroine; and *The Great Train Robbery* (1979), mildly amusing Victoriana that pays laudable attention to such period foibles as dog-rat fights. Writer Robert Benton launched his career behind the camera with *Bad Company* (1972), co-authored by David Newman, his collaborator on the script of *Bonnie and Clyde* (1967). This Civil War "shaggy dog" story, with its juvenile stars, rambled too widely for most audiences. Benton's *The Late Show* (1977) proved a surprise hit, however, exploiting the screen chemistry that developed between Art Carney, an actor who discovered a second career in the Seventies, and Lily Tomlin, the most imaginative comedienne of the era, the queen of shopping-bag ladies. *Kramer vs. Kramer* (1979), which Benton adapted from Avery Corman's best seller, and filmed in insistent close-ups by Nestor Almendros, also depends quite heavily on the charm of Dustin Hoffman as Ted and the power of Meryl Streep as Joanna to uncover the deeper resonances in a child custody suit.

No writer-turned-director in the Seventies generated more excitement, plaudits, or derision than Peter Bogdanovich, film critic-turned-film maker. *Targets* (1968), his auspicious debut, saw its promise confirmed in *The Last Picture Show* (1971), a masterful adaptation of Larry McMurtry's first-rate novel, lovingly photographed in black and white by Robert Surtees and produced by Bert Schneider's ambitious BBS productions. Bogdanovich coaxes exquisite performances from Timothy Bottoms as a boy on the verge of manhood, and from Oscar-winner Ben Johnson as Sam the Lion, his mentor, and fellow Oscar-winner Cloris Leachman as a desperate, lonely, sex-starved older woman. After a fine documentary on one of his Hollywood idols, *Directed by John Ford* (1971), Bogdanovich turned to screwball comedy in *What's Up, Doc?* (1972), with Barbra Streisand and Ryan O'Neal as mismatched lovers. *Paper Moon* (1973) was buoyed by the mugging of Tatum O'Neal and the bumptious good humor of Madeline Kahn as Trixie Delight, but even Verna Fields's editing could not conceal the many uninspired patches. Audiences and critics loathed *Daisy Miller* (1974), a Cybill Shepherd vehicle quite faithful to Henry James's novella and considerably better than its reviews. *At Long Last Love* (1975), a Cole Porter musical starring Burt Reynolds, proved a concept just as bad as it sounds. Bogdanovich later admitted he did not know how to make sophisticated song and dance numbers work, and the film is justly included on most lists of the ten worst films ever made. Star Burt Reynolds disparages *At Long Last Love* and Bogdanovich every chance he gets, and the final sequence in Reynolds' film about stuntmen, *Hooper* (1978), features a none-too-subtle putdown of a director who pontificates about "pieces of time," the title of Bogdanovich's collected film criticism. Bogdanovich's *Nickleodon* (1976), an enthralling treatment of the patent wars that disrupted the early days of silent films, failed to find an audience, and he turned his energies to smaller projects. *Saint Jack* (1979) was his powerful comeback, a sensitive adaptation of Paul Theroux's novel, featuring Ben Gazzara as Jack Flowers, one of the finest characterizations of the decade. *Saint Jack* is Bogdanovich's

Timothy Bottoms and Ben Johnson in Peter Bogdanovich's THE LAST PICTURE SHOW (1971).

Cybill Shepherd in Peter Bogdanovich's DAISY MILLER (1974).

Burt Reynolds as Michael Oliver Pritchard III in Peter Bogdanovich's ill fated AT LONG LAST LOVE (1975).

Vietnam film, an understated but devastating commentary on the corruption at the center of America's Far East adventure.

The biggest Vietnam film of the Seventies, *Apocalypse Now* (1979), directed by "movie brat" Francis (Ford) Coppola, won the Grand Prize at the Cannes Film Festival, ending the decade on an American victory just as *M*A*S*H*, Altman's Korean comedy, had begun it. Francis Coppola, who dropped his middle name as the decade unfolded, was the reigning power, the motivating force behind a youthful takeover of big budget projects. When Billy Wilder's protagonist in *Fedora* (1978), Barry Detweiler (William Holden), laments that his Old Hollywood has been taken over by "the kids with beards," he obviously means the three major new talents of the Seventies: University of California at Los Angeles film school's Francis Coppola, University of Southern California film school's George Lucas, and Steven Spielberg, who left California State at Long Beach to occupy an office at Universal.

Steven Spielberg may be the most commercially viable talent in America today. He quickly graduated from the *Colombo* series to a spate of extraordinary telefilms, including *Duel* (1971), an anguished battle of wits between man and machine, eventually acclaimed in the movie theaters of Europe. Then came *Sugarland Express* (1973), a chase caper with a vivacious Goldie Hawn as a mother who wants her baby back so badly she is willing to free her husband (William Atherton) from prison, kidnap a policeman (Michael Sacks), and defy local vigilantes along her route, until her adventures lay siege to the media. As in many of the *Bonnie and Clyde* influenced adventures of the Seventies (*Badlands*, 1973; *Outlaw Blues*, 1977; *The Gauntlet*, 1977; *Convoy*, 1978), the media reaction to this drive for individual freedom becomes the real focus in *Sugarland Express*. Spielberg explores the way "media can determine the outcome of a public event." *Jaws* was Spielberg's own media event, a blockbuster that gobbled up all the competition so effectively that Universal did not release another major film in the summer of 1975. *Close Encounters of the Third Kind* exploded on screens in 1977; its colossal mothership proved a magnet attracting viewers to Devil's Tower and the box office. Spielberg's new wealth allowed him to produce Bob Zemeckis' *I Wanna Hold Your Hand* (1978), a neglected but accomplished reverie about frenzied teen-age reactions to the Beatles' arrival in America, and

Robert Shaw, Roy Scheider, and Richard Dreyfuss in Steven Spielberg's JAWS (1975).

Matthew Robbins' romance *Continental Divide*. At decade's end deals were underway joining Spielberg and Lucas in a major action drama for Paramount. This widely discussed project, *Raiders of the Lost Ark*, began with the provisos that there would be a minimum of four sequels, that Steven Spielberg would direct, and that George Lucas would serve as executive producer. Paramount assumed a major part of the production costs in a deal most outsiders saw as unfavorable to the studio. Paramount president Mike Eisner defended his position stoutly, however: "We are totally confident we will realize a tremendous return on our investment. You don't make standard deals with these kinds of people. People assume that to get Lucas and Spielberg together you'd have to give them the lot and your first born."

Universal and Columbia cooperated in the production of *1941* (1979), Spielberg's playful combination of "*Mad, Mad, Mad World* and Daffy Duck," set in Los Angeles six days after Pearl Harbor. Spielberg intended *1941* as a "stupidly outrageous . . . celebration of paranoia," and chose a cast calculated to intensify the mayhem of an alleged sneak attack, including the wayward sergeant Dan Aykroyd down in the streets and the mad pilot John Belushi up in the sky. Audiences and critics found *1941* curiously unfunny and elephantine.

George Lucas began the decade with *THX1138* (1970), a misunderstood expansion of his University of Southern California award-winning short, *Electronic Labyrinth*, produced by Coppola's American Zeotrope; a scary "allegory with a touch of cubism," *THX1138* alienated Warner Brothers executives, who foolishly canceled all further projects with Lucas and Coppola. *American Graffiti* (1973), scripted by Lucas and Gloria Katz and Willard Huyck, was made using a controversial two-camera system at a cost of only 750,000 dollars, yet it grossed over 55 million dollars domestically, generating a sequel, *More American Graffiti* (1979). The original, Lucas's rock music "sociology plus nostalgia," helped the careers of Richard Dreyfuss (*Jaws*, 1975; *Close Encounters*, 1977; *The Goodbye Girl*, 1978), Harrison Ford (*Star Wars*, 1977), Kathleen Quinlan (*I Never Promised You a Rose Garden*, 1978; *The Runner Stumbles*, 1979), Candy Clark (*The Man Who Fell to Earth*, 1976; *Handle with Care*, 1978; *The Big Sleep*, 1978), and television personalities Ron Howard, Suzanne Somers, and MacKenzie Phillips. *Star Wars*

Richard Dreyfuss in Steven Spielberg's CLOSE ENCOUNTERS OF THE THIRD KIND (1977).

Paul LeMat and MacKenzie Phillips in George Lucas' AMERICAN GRAFFITI (1973).

(1977), Lucas' megafilm, showed once and for all that he could deal with science fiction as popular entertainment. For all his gargantuan successes, however, Lucas maintains his commitment to personal films: "I identify totally with Thex, struggling out from a benevolent and disintegrating environment; I wasted four years of my life cruisin' like the kids in *Graffiti,* and I'm now on an intergalactic dream of heroism. I'm telling the story of me, and—who knows?—it might set a trend."

Francis Coppola has a similar vision of cinema as an extension of his own life and will. Between his two *Godfather* films, he took time to script and direct his own award-winning variant on *Blow Up* (1967): *The Conversation* (1974), with Gene Hackman as Harry Caul, a surveillance man whose privacy is ravished. Like the Nixon of Watergate, Harry is destroyed by an obsession he cannot control or understand. Coppola's own obsession for the rest of the decade was *Apocalypse Now* (1979), his attempt to update Joseph Conrad's *Heart of Darkness* in the jungles of Vietnam. The script by John Milius was first prepared in 1967, and announced in 1974 as a ten million dollar project; by its release time, problems in the location shooting had made costs soar, and Coppola had mortgaged his possessions to complete the final editing. Set in 1968, *Apocalypse Now* stars Marlon Brando as Colonel Kurtz, who has established himself as a god in his Cambodian outpost, and Martin Sheen as Captain Willard, the West Point graduate on a "search and destroy" mission. Robert Duvall plays Lt. Colonel Kilgore, a mad tyrant who has his men surf in the middle of a battlefield and who leads helicopter attacks to the strains of Wagner's "Die Walküre." Even Coppola admits *Apocalypse Now* is operatic; at Cannes press conferences, he explained that his "unfinished project" was "more an experience than a movie": "At the beginning there's a story. Along the river the story becomes less important and the experience more important."

Francis Ford Coppola celebrated his fortieth birthday and the tenth anniversary of the founding of American Zoetrope on the weekend of April 14, 1979, at his Napa Valley winery. According to *Village Voice* accounts, brass bands played "Happy Birthday," dumpy cheerleaders chanted "Francis has the power, Francis has the power," while the revelers, including Coppola, Robert De Niro, Dennis Hopper,

Gene Hackman in Francis Coppola's THE CONVERSATION (1974).

Wim Wenders, and George Lucas, joined in the chorus "We will rule Hollywood, we will rule Hollywood, we will rule Hollywood." For the movie brats, "*that's* what it's all about."

4. Do Ya Think I'm Sexy?

> *"Mr. Laemmle,"* I once asked, *"what do you think is the most important element in the success or failure of a picture?"*
> The answer came back at once. *"The right actors in the right parts or the wrong actors in the wrong parts."*
> GARSON KANIN, *Hollywood*

IF, AS MICHAEL ARLEN has suggested, the Academy Awards ceremonies are the royal pageants of democracy, playful yet courtly and aristocratic promenades choreographed for the edification of the masses, then there has been no more moving or noble moment in their history than the 1979 entrance of the aged Duke of Hollywood, John Wayne. Long a symbol of Americanism and masculinity, Wayne was fighting his last battle with cancer, and all the audience and spectators for his final public appearance were as excited by his courage as they were shocked by his physical decline. The man who had made the first major Vietnam film in Hollywood, the hawkish *Green Berets* (1968), was in Los Angeles that night to announce the best picture of the year. Though it looked for a while that Wayne might end up embracing his nemesis, Jane Fonda, star of *Coming Home* (1978), one of the nominated films, when he finally quieted the applause for his personal heroism and "moved 'em out," the winner was *The Deer Hunter*, a film closer in spirit to Wayne's well-publicized conservative defense of "The Republic."

Most movie fans would rather remember the Duke as he was earlier, perhaps even as he was in *True Grit* (1969), which won him the first best actor award presented in the Seventies. Who could forget the aged Marshal Rooster Cogburn confronting four mounted outlaws at the edge of a birch grove? Or his startling command when they refused to surrender: "Fill your hand, you sonuvabitch!" It was "bold talk for a one-eyed fat man," yet at the end of the encounter, four renegades lay dead, and Rooster Cogburn needed only regret the death of his horse Bo.

97

John Wayne was both the tallest and oldest of the old guard of Hollywood actors who survived the upheavals and traumas of the Sixties and Seventies. The camera is not kind to older heroes, so traditional Hollywood wisdom suggests that fifty is a good age for leading men to consider new roles in films, either as character actors or as producers and directors. Big stars like George C. Scott, Marlon Brando, Paul Newman, Jack Lemmon, and Walter Matthau all turned fifty in the Seventies, but John Wayne was the *eminence gris,* over seventy when he finally claimed his self-chosen epitaph, *feo, fuerte y formal:* "he was ugly, he was strong and he had dignity."

Many of John Wayne's last films were purely genre exercises, though *Rio Lobo* (1970) did profit from the direction of Howard Hawks, while *The Cowboys* (1972) added a new vulnerability to his characterization in a startling death scene, and *Rooster Cogburn* (1975), the sequel to *True Grit,* gave him a chance to play opposite Katherine Hepburn. Wayne explored the urban plains as a detective in John Sturges' surprisingly effective *McQ* (1974), and even left his home sod for a quirkier, London-based detective adventure, *Brannigan* (1975). Wayne's best film in the Seventies, however, was *The Shootist,* lovingly directed by the king of the action film, Don Siegel. This lean, nostalgic tale of a Nineteenth Century gunfighter who visits a doctor (James Stewart) in Carson City, Nevada, the first year of the Twentieth Century to discover that he faces a horrible death from cancer features resonant performances by Lauren Bacall as the woman who shelters him and Richard Boone as a visitor who haunts him. At the center, however is John Bernard Books, Wayne's tortured gunman, prematurely aged, frightened by mortality, and racked by spasmodic pain. The personal echoes are obvious to any viewer; Wayne the actor and Books the adventurer each conceal the same fatal cancer in a remarkable show of personal dignity. Bernard Books's final shoot-out at the Metropole Cafe is John Wayne's final performance, the capstone of a stunning career spanning five decades.

John Wayne's dramatic appearance at the 1979 Academy Awards ceremony contrasts ironically with the unsettling decision of the 1970 winner for best performance by an actor, George C. Scott, to refuse the Oscar. The iconoclastic Scott argued that such competitions degraded the profession of acting, and asked that his characterization be appraised purely on its own merits. Scott had one of the longest and

*John Wayne in Don Siegel's **THE SHOOTIST** (1976).*

most difficult assignments of the decade in *Patton* (1970). He was on screen, center stage, from his first bombastic tirade in front of the flag to the very bitter end; for this larger-than-life general, war is all and peace "a veritable hell." *Patton* was scripted by Francis Coppola, who won an Oscar, although he was convinced his hero was "obviously nuts." Rather than glorifying Patton, Coppola tried to turn him into a "man out of his time, a pathetic hero, a Don Quixote figure." Instead of the war epic it originally planned, Twentieth Century-Fox had a three-hour-long epic characterization: a tight-fisted, cigar-chomping Little Caesar, replete with pearl-handled pistols, five stars, and Napoleonic ambition. Craggy-faced Scott makes all Patton's mad visions seem real and his classic poetry come alive; his arm quivers in salutes just as it explodes across the face of a malingering private. For all the external explosions and bombings, it is the energy inside, Patton's intensity of conviction, and his will to power that illuminate the screen. No wonder *Patton* was the film Richard Nixon screened the night before he announced the invasion of Cambodia; megalomania is always its own best friend.

Even a refused Oscar means new bargaining power for an actor, and George C. Scott's career affords a fine case study of how heightened independence fostered both artistic achievement and excessive self-indulgence in the Seventies. The publicity and recognition made George C. Scott bankable; despite faltering box-office appeal, he remained one of Hollywood's busiest actors. The year after the Oscar, for example, he appeared in three extraordinarily fine projects. *The Last Run* (1971), Richard Fleischer's gangster in exile melodrama, scripted by Alan Sharp and photographed by Sven Nykvist, presents Scott as Harry Garmes, a tired but competent warrior, a dedicated professional in a nihilistic age. Like so many of Scott's characterizations, Harry elicits grudging respect and understanding; his weariness and disenchantment seem rather noble in the face of a world in collapse. He is the gangster as tragic hero *par excellence;* he no longer belongs in Chicago or in his Portuguese fishing village. Justin Playfair, the New Yorker in *They Might Be Giants* (1971), another man out of sync with contemporary mores, swears he really lives at 221 Baker Street; his Watson (Joanne Woodward) is an analyst who falls in love with his illusion, following him gladly as he stalks the streets in Inverness cape and Deerstalker cap, seeking a climactic

100

George C. Scott and Karl Malden in Franklin Schaffner's PATTON (1970).

showdown with Moriarty. Although the film was too whimsical for most audiences, the clever script by playwright James Goldman and dreamy photography by Victor Kemper make this vision of paranoia quite engrossing. Paddy Chayefsky's literate script for *The Hospital* (1971) also gave Scott plenty of room for remarkable histrionics. As Dr. Herbert Bock, he lashes out at the restraints and perversities of modern civilization; in a key confrontation with Barbara Drummond (Diana Rigg) all his atavistic rage breaks through terrifyingly. Bock's psychic torments are much darker and more dreadful than the murderous antics of Barbara's father, yet Scott manages masterfully to make his distraught doctor a sympathetic, almost paternal figure in a universe gone wildly awry.

Suicidal depression also haunts the paternal Kilninsky in *The New Centurions* (1972), a startlingly bleak study of cops in a decadent society, based on Joseph Wambaugh's novel. As Mase in *Oklahoma Crude* (1973), Scott dons long underwear and suspenders to join Faye Dunaway in her futile war against oil monopolies; the heavy handed direction of Stanley Kramer marred an otherwise interesting project. Director Mike Nichols did not do much better for the immensely disappointing *Day of the Dolphin* (1973). None of Scott's loving posturing as Dr. Jake Terrell was enough to save Buck Henry's script about dolphins who talk and clumsy assassination conspiracies. Dolphins may live in a constant state of ecstasy, but the cast of this film seems lost in a state of confusion, wondering whether they are in an enlightened documentary, juvenile fantasy, or lurid soap opera.

Bank Shot (1975), directed by Gower Champion and based on the novel by Donald E. Westlake, features Scott as Walter Ballantine, the ultimate disenfranchised convict who decides to steal a bank rather than to rob it. Scott obviously enjoys this whacky role and even dons an outrageous hippy disguise to scoot along on a motorcycle in this very graceful box-office failure. *The Hindenburg* (1975) lacked all charm; this inflated bomb squanders the talents of everyone aboard, especially Scott. *Islands in the Stream* (1977), directed by Franklin Schaffner, contains one of Scott's finest portrayals as Thomas Hudson, the alienated artist, yet all his carefully nuanced acting cannot conceal the unconscious self-parody of Hemingway's novel. Paul Schrader's *Hardcore* (1978) also suffers slightly from stylization,

102

George C. Scott and Jack Palance in Stanley Kramer's OKLAHOMA CRUDE (1973).

George C. Scott in Franklin Schaffner's ISLANDS IN THE STREAM (1977).

though Scott's silent tears as he watches his daughter in a pornographic short are overpowering. Scott also shines in Stanley Donen's *Movie Movie* (1978), an affectionate tribute to double features and the Warner Brothers backlot. Scott mugs beautifully as fight manager Gloves Malone, clutches his failing heart movingly as Broadway promoter Spats Baxter, and smiles devilishly in the mock coming attraction for *Zero Hour,* a vision of "war at its best."

Like many aging actors, George C. Scott also tried his hand at directing. *Rage* (1972), an impassioned sermonette about chemical warfare and industrial pollutants, was quickly sold to television. *The Savage Is Loose* (1974), an updated Swiss Family Robinson adventure fraught with Oedipal tensions, played its only extended engagement at a New York City theater Scott rented. He had hoped to sell copies of the film outright to exhibitors and break forever the stranglehold of distributors, but the film proved so unpopular that the projectionist often ran it without arc light to empty houses. Scott lost over a quarter million dollars in a year of exhibiting *The Savage Is Loose,* but he refused to be silenced, just as he refused his Oscar.

On March 27, 1973, another Oscar for best actor was declined by an Apache maiden in tribal attire, Sacheen Littlefeather, who told presenter Liv Ullmann and the Academy that Marlon Brando declined any award from an industry with a history of insulting American Indians. Brando, the dedicated method actor who turned into a superstar bigger than any of his roles, spent the early part of the decade in artistic though noncommercial endeavors. Gillo Pontecorvo's dazzling *Burn!* (or *Queimada!*) (1970), which highlights his compelling portrait of *agent provocateur* Sir William Walker in Queimada, remains one of the decade's neglected masterpieces. Walker is a man obsessed with power, a manipulator who sees the Third World as his own playground, whether he is establishing revolutionary heroes or burning the island on the orders of sugar merchants. Crazed by guilt, yet swollen by pride, only an assassin's knife finally deflates his ego. Peter Quint in *The Nightcomers* (1972), Michael Winner's imaginative prelude to the action in Henry James's *Turn of the Screw,* is the consummate sadist, whose bondage games with Miss Jessel (Stephanie Beacham) provide Miles (Christopher Ellis) and Flora (Verna Harvey) ample inspiration for grisly deeds. As Quint, Brando mesmerizes the children with an extemporized tall tale

Marlon Brando in Gillo Pontecorvo's BURN! (1970).

about his scalawag father, which foreshadows his psychoanalytic improvisations as Paul in Bernardo Bertolucci's controversial essay on male sexuality, *Last Tango in Paris* (1973). Many critics complained that Brando was never nude in this adult psychodrama, while his co-star Maria Schneider was constantly stripped naked and manipulated. Brando's long reveries, however, about his alcoholic father, poetic mother, and the cow dung that stuck to him throughout his youth lay Paul bare in ways unparalleled in modern cinema. Brando and Bertolucci have both spoken at length about the shattering process of self-discovery in this project.

The Godfather (1972) resulted in Brando's Oscar for a performance every actor in America must have envied. When Brando tested for the role of the don, he so transformed his appearance that few observers recognized him on screen. During the filming itself, Francis Coppola noted, Brando complemented technique with "a full flush of intuition," always reacting in character. His delicate stroking of the cat, stiff manners, and awkward clowning with his grandchildren are classic examples of a subtle art. Brando proved just as adept in Arthur Penn's ill-fated Western, *The Missouri Breaks* (1976), brilliantly conceived by Thomas McGuane. As "regulator" Robert E. Lee Clayton, Brando affects an Irish brogue, dons several outlandish outfits including a woman's dress, and takes one of the most amusing baths in cinema history. Even alone on a desolate plain with his horse, this plunderer is a poet, warbling love songs full of Salome and Cleopatra; Brando more than lives up to McGuane's only description of Clayton, "weird as weird can be," which proved an equally adept summary of the mass audience's judgment of the film. *Superman* (1978) helped Brando maintain his retreat at Tatieroa in style, while *Apocalypse Now* (1979) reestablished his artistic credentials as the godfather of tinseltown.

Major stars were deluged with scripts in the Seventies, and their approval could "greenlight" a project. Some performers, however, like Paul Newman, often seemed at a loss to select material suited to their talents. *WUSA* (1970), Newman's choice as "the most significant film I've ever made and the best," does have a fine script by Robert Stone based on his celebrated novel *A Hall of Mirrors*, but the lead character, Rheinhardt, is too thoroughly cynical to elicit sympathy. This glib radio announcer's last comment, "I'm a survivor.

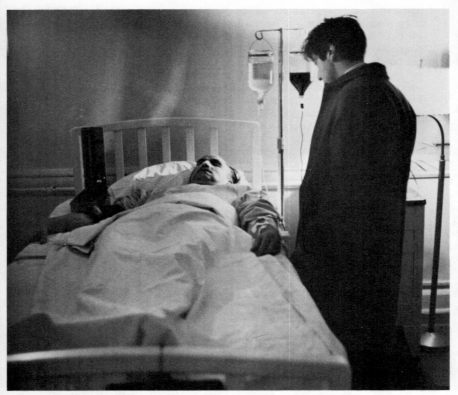

Marlon Brando and Al Pacino in Francis Coppola's THE GODFATHER (1972).

108

Marlon Brando in Arthur Penn's THE MISSOURI BREAKS (1976).

Ain't that great?'' suggests the somber mood this saga of a right-wing New Orleans radio station creates; Newman's good looks just do not fit the role. Similarly, *Sometimes a Great Notion* (1971) fails not because of Ken Kesey's anti-union narrative or Newman's inexperience as a director; it flounders instead on the tension between Newman's natural charm and his character Hank's pigheaded "never give an inch" individualism. In *Pocket Money* (1972) Newman almost chokes on all the pregnant pauses; he is an upbeat talent in a downbeat film. Even in *The Life and Times of Judge Roy Bean* (1972), one of John Huston's better Seventies offerings, Newman is required to act behind a scraggly beard, scarred with sunburn, and finally gray with age; these impositions seem to dull the blue of his eyes. Huston even has Newman playing second fiddle to a beer-guzzling bear named Bruno. *The Macintosh Man* (1973), another Huston opus, seems more concerned with the mechanics of auto chases in Ireland and visuals of swimming near Malta than with the trials of protagonist Rearden. *The Sting* (1973), Newman's best role of the decade, clearly subordinated characterization to its elaborate plot. *The Towering Inferno* (1974) was purely a celebrity cameo, while *The Drowning Pool* (1975) submerged Newman's energies in an inhospitable role as hardboiled private eye Lew Harper. *Buffalo Bill and the Indians* (1971) and *Quintet* (1979) proved two of Robert Altman's least accessible works, just as Newman's own production of *The Effects of Gamma Rays on Man-in-the-Moon Marigolds* (1972), starring his wife Joanne Woodward and based on Paul Zindel's Pulitzer Prize-winning play, mystified audiences. There were many rumors that Paul Newman was planning to play an older homosexual track coach enamored of his young male protégé, but *Slapshot* (1977), which cast him as a Machiavellian hockey coach in the bush leagues, shocked audiences only with its profane language. Coach Reggie Dunlop was just another scabrous middle-aged male chauvinist, who had taken one too many punches, inhaled one too many bottles of Jack Daniels, and slept with one too many married woman. Actor Newman himself played a surfeit of poor roles in the Seventies.

Jack Lemmon also threatened to burn himself out in the Seventies; only his Achilles heel was roles which were far too similar. It is virtually impossible to separate the romantic klutzes in *The April Fools* (1969), *The Out of Towners* (1970), *The War Between Men and*

110

Paul Newman in George Roy Hill's SLAPSHOT (1977).

Women (1972), and *Avanti* (1972); even *Save the Tiger* (1972) involves the same schlemiel with a bit more sensitivity. Both *The Front Page* (1974) and *The Entertainer* (1975) are badly flawed remakes; *The Prisoner of Second Avenue* (1975) is weak Neil Simon, and *Airport '77* tepid schlock. Only *Alex and the Gypsy* (1976), John Korty's quaint little sleeper, and *The China Syndrome* (1979) suggested what a big talent Lemmon was squandering. As Jack Godell in James Bridges' topical blockbuster, Lemmon steals the show from both Jane Fonda and Michael Douglas; the drama shifts from the world of media hype to the agonies of one little man who knows "we're losing control" of the nuclear reactor, a loss that Dr. Lowell (Donald Hotton) prophetically declares could "render an area the size of Pennsylvania permanently uninhabitable." The subsequent events at Three Mile Island helped cement Lemmon's performance in audience memories.

Walter Matthau, another prince in Hollywood's old guard, played it safe in the Seventies, sticking mostly to surefire material like Neil Simon plays (*Plaza Suite*, 1971; *The Sunshine Boys*, 1975; and *California Suite*, 1978), celebrity blockbusters (*Earthquake*, 1974), and presold properties (*The Taking of Pelham One Two Three*, 1974). While Matthau gravitated towards the sentimental in films like *Pete 'n Tillie* (1972), *The Bad News Bears* (1976), and *Casey's Shadow* (1977), his very best performances came in the gritty *The Last Policeman* (1973) and in Don Siegel's offbeat Mafia yarn, *Charley Varrick* (1972). As Varrick, Matthau brings good humor to a convoluted tale of bungled robberies, desperate escapes, and jumbled lives: Michael Butler's camera uncannily reinforces the understated, wry social comment in this character study of "the last of the independents" trapped in a world where even mobsters and whores are organized, and where the natural has been replaced by the plastic.

As Hollywood's senior actors struggled to find mature images of masculinity, a new breed of macho hero stampeded onto the screen, led by the irrepressibly popular Burt Reynolds. Much of the time, these performers paid scant attention to the value of their material; everything hinged on a lucrative deal. Reynolds, for example, could move from his sensitive, studied characterization of Lewis in John Boorman's cerebral adaptation of a James Dickey novel, *Deliverance* (1972), to mindless drive-in specials like *White Lightning* (1973), *Gator* (1976), and *Hooper* (1978). Only after his box-office reputation

Jack Lemmon, Michael Douglas, and Jane Fonda in James Bridges' THE CHINA SYNDROME (1979).

Robby Benson and Burt Reynolds in director Reynolds' THE END (1978).

was established by hits like *The Longest Yard* (1974) and *Smokey and the Bandit* (1977) did Reynolds turn to more challenging material like Michael Ritchie's insightful *Semi-Tough* (1977) and *Starting Over* (1979), Alan Pakula's influential study of male menopause.

Clint Eastwood, another macho maverick, also stayed close to his audience's expectations in shoot 'em ups like *Joe Kidd* (1972), *The High Plains Drifter* (1972), and *The Outlaw Josey Wales* (1976). *The Gauntlet* (1977) was just a tired variation of his Dirty Harry series; only *Thunderbolt and Lightfoot* (1974), directed and written by Michael Cimino, brought new insights to the cops and robbers genre. *Every Which Way but Loose* (1978), an immensely profitable undertaking, stands as an epic example of what disorganized, mindless drivel can excite the denizens of Yumpsville. Eastwood's last film of the decade, *Escape from Alcatraz* (1979), suggests that even he sees the need for a change. Compared to his earlier films, it is the work of a man with a "superior I.Q." which escapes all his earlier artistic straitjackets. Eastwood sorely needs strong directors like Don Siegel to employ his lean acting style effectively; his self-directed projects are not auteurish but amateurish.

Ex-marine Steve McQueen, one-time star of *Wanted Dead or Alive,* tried to escape the macho stereotype in his adaptation of Ibsen's *An Enemy of the People* (1976), but his most memorable projects in the Seventies depend more on brawn than brains. *Junior Bonner* (1972) and *The Getaway* (1972) are typical Peckinpah fare, while *The Towering Inferno* (1974) is pure Irwin Allen. McQueen's performance was tremendous in the grueling *Papillon* (1973), but this adventure film proved far too harrowing for American tastes.

Charles Bronson, another of the moneyed macho males of the Seventies, first appeared in undistinguished, imitation *film noir* capers like *The Family* (1971), *The Mechanic* (1972), *The Valachi Papers* (1972), and *The Stone Killer* (1973), all long on gore and short on sense. Then Michael Winner's *Death Wish* (1974), an urban nightmare of rape and retaliation, hit a responsive chord among yahoos who would like to see repression grow from the barrel of a gun; its brand of vigilante justice fueled a rising tide of fascism in America. Bronson followed this with a fine characterization of a cagey street fighter in the hard-hitting period piece, *Hard Times* (1975); a better-than-average portrayal in a poetic Western, *From Noon Till Three*

Clint Eastwood in Don Siegel's ESCAPE FROM ALCATRAZ (1979).

Charles Bronson in Michael Winner's DEATH WISH (1974).

(1976); and a most impressive performance as a Russian agent in Don Siegel's tense *Telefon* (1977). None of these parts pleased his fans, however, and after a best-forgotten role in Dino De Laurentiis' ghastly answer to *Jaws, The White Buffalo* (1978), Bronson announced the inevitable sequel, *Death Wish II,* the further adventures of business-man-turned-executioner Paul Kersey.

Some muscular Hollywood heroes tried to soften their image enough to suggest some sensitivity and grace. Nick Nolte, for exam-ple, forsook the pretty-boy heroics of *The Deep* (1977) for the hypnot-ic zen of *Who'll Stop the Rain* (1978), Karel Reisz's magnificent adaptation of Robert Stone's National Book Award-winning novel, *Dog Soldiers* (the film's title in Britain). This searing portrait of 1971 America, awash in guilt, despair, and drugs, haunted by Vietnam, and policed by marauders, allows Nolte to demonstrate his control of precise phrasing and studied diction without eliminating entirely his acrobatics. So, too, *North Dallas Forty* (1979), though it lingers long in locker rooms and on football fields, also shows Nolte the thinker, dreamer, and romantic. *Heart Beat* (1980), written and directed by John Byrum, may not have pleased visionary poet Allen Ginsburg, but Nolte expands his horizons in this biography of the Beat Genera-tion's legendary saint, Neal Cassady, opposite John Heard as peripatetic novelist Jack Kerouac and Sissy Spacek as Carolyn Cas-sady.

Handsome Kris Kristofferson also assayed some complex roles demanding sweetness and light as well as strength. Once a loner and drifter (*Cisco Pike,* 1971; *Pat Garrett and Billy the Kid,* 1973), Kris-tofferson emerged as one of the great lovers of the decade, enchanting Susan Anspach in *Blume in Love* (1973), comforting Ellen Burstyn in *Alice Doesn't Live Here Anymore* (1975), seducing Sarah Miles in the torrid *Sailor Who Fell From Grace with the Sea* (1976), and captivat-ing Ali MacGraw in *Convoy* (1978). Kristofferson's charms were so considerable that he was drafted to play John Norman Howard in former hairdresser Jon Peters' ode to Barbra Streisand, *A Star Is Born* (1976), an overdubbed remake that devoured scriptwriters and performers alike. Kristofferson claims he was in an alcoholic daze throughout the production; all that survives in anyone's memory of the debacle is Streisand's curtain call, "Evergreen," one of the longest, most emotionally overcharged takes in film history. Fortunately, Michael Ritchie's *Semi-Tough* (1977) helped cure Kristofferson's hangover, as he wooed Barbara Jane Bookman (Jill Clayburgh) under the watchful eye of macho roommate Billy Clyde Pluckett (Burt Reynolds).

All the great romantic leads in the Seventies softened the macho mold considerably. They were not sissies exactly, but few would have launched a suicidal charge across the sands of Iwo Jima or shot it out at O.K. Corral. Seventies matinee idols were generally urban types, a bit on the short side, with broad smiles, mottled complexions, penetrating eyes, and mild neuroses. They were not so charming and genteel as Cary Grant, nor so lithe and aristocratic as Fred Astaire; they lacked Bogie's panache and Gable's rakishness. If anything, their very ordinariness, a sort of puckish charm, made Richard Dreyfuss, Dustin Hoffman, and Elliott Gould household names; even the better-looking heroes—Robert Redford, John Travolta, and Warren Beatty—all paraded their weaknesses just as boldly as they flashed their profiles.

Robert Redford, a forty year old who kept young women swooning in the aisles, publicly renounced the whole sex god trip and conscientiously sought out complex roles in major productions like his electrifyingly beautiful *Jeremiah Johnson* (1972), the overly elegant *Great Gatsby* (1974), and the charmingly understated *Great Waldo Pepper* (1975). Like Kristofferson, Redford was badly bruised in his one bout with superstar Barbra Streisand, *The Way We Were* (1973), a romance set in Hollywood during the Red Scare that missed many splendid opportunities to treat serious questions; his romance with Faye Dunaway in *Three Days of the Condor* (1975) was similarly lacking in conviction. Redford was the driving force, however, behind *All the President's Men* (1976), a bold political and artistic statement, and the decade ended with his memorably rich performance as the aging cowboy Sonny Steele in *The Electric Horseman* (1979), director Sydney Pollack's dazzling satire of "The Marlboro Man meeting Barbara Walters." Tired of being duped and packaged, Steele makes his charge for freedom astride the abused thoroughbred champion, Running Star, only to find meaning, laughter, and love with an educated, liberated reporter played by Jane Fonda.

One problem all the new male movie idols of the Seventies faced was the lack of role models; as critic-turned-filmmaker Pauline Kael

Elliott Gould, Diane Keaton, Warren Berlinger, and Victoria Principal at a sex clinic in Norman Panama's I WILL, I WILL . . . FOR NOW (1975).

astutely observed, "Nobody understands what contemporary heroes or heroines should be, or how they should relate to each other. . . ." A young performer like John Travolta could mime the past in hits like *Carrie* (1976) or *Grease* (1978) or even suggest the loneliness of the present in *Saturday Night Fever* (1977), but when he turned to love in modern society opposite rising star Lily Tomlin in *Moment by Moment* it seemed, as *Variety* noted, "like hours and hours." When gigolo Strip (Travolta) tells his older paramour Trisha (Tomlin), "If you're not ready to commit to a meaningful relationship with me, that's it, I've had it with cheap sex," audiences laughed uproariously. Meaningful relationships and cheap sex seemed miles from the earlier formula, "I love you." The movies had managed, like the society around them, to fulfill Lana Turner's immortal lament, "They've taken the romance out of sex."

Richard Dreyfuss had his fling at sex without romance in the X-rated "degenerate film, with dignity," *Inserts* (1975), John Byrum's first feature as writer and director, which was produced in England though it treated the anguish of a washed-up director and has-been silent-screen queen filming pornography in Hollywood in the Thirties. Brilliant porno or not, *Inserts* proved too involuted and arcane for American audiences, just as Dreyfuss' Canadian tour de force, *The Apprenticeship of Duddy Kravitz* (1974) seemed too bleak and ethnic. Huge successes in *American Graffiti* (1973), *Jaws* (1975), and *Close Encounters of the Third Kind* (1977), however, paved the way to Dreyfuss' Oscar nomination for his performance in *The Goodbye Girl* (1978), directed by Herbert Ross and scripted by Neil Simon. As Elliott Garfield, Dreyfuss has all the lines an actor could dream of: he banters with Paula McFadden (Marsha Mason) then beds her, wisecracks with precocious Lucy McFadden (Quinn Cummings) then adopts her, all as he limns an outrageous portrait of a sensitive actor stuck in a production of *Richard III* done in drag. This role proved such a plum that a proposed sequel was canceled in favor of a television series, centered on Elliott, extending the role of the actor as he moves into the family and his professional life changes. *The Big Fix* (1978), directed by Jeremy Paul Kagan, is just as centered on Dreyfuss' portrayal of Moses Gunn, a one-time activist forced to relive the lost revolution of the Sixties and to reenact a tragic romance.

John Travolta in Jane Wagner's MOMENT BY MOMENT (1979).

Richard Dreyfuss and Marsha Mason in Herbert Ross' THE GOODBYE GIRL (1978).

Like Dreyfuss, Dustin Hoffman was such a success (in *The Graduate*, 1967, and *Midnight Cowboy*, 1969) that he soon found himself trying to carry whole movies singlehandedly. Arthur Penn's *Little Big Man* (1970), from Thomas Berger's picaresque Western, ranged far too widely to allow Jack Crabb, its one-hundred-and-eleven-year-old narrator, "a liar of insane proportions," to come into focus, just as *Who's Harry Kellerman and Why Is He Saying These Terrible Things About Me?* (1971) concentrated too intensely on a schizophrenia better captured in the choppy paragraphs of Herb Gardner's story. Hoffman was suitably savage in Peckinpah's bloody *Straw Dogs* (1971), clumsy as could be in *Alfredo-Alfredo* (1972), and devastatingly effective in the challenging *Papillon* (1973), but *Lenny* (1974) was his big role, the perfect casting every performer dreams of. Hoffman lived and breathed the persona of Lenny Bruce; director Bob Fosse needed only move his camera in close and adjust the lighting to record a professional at the peak of his art. The courtroom harangues, the intimate nightclub routines, and the checkered romance with Honey (Valerie Perrine) each present another facet of the clown-turned-martyr. Hoffman's portrait of America's king of fools, our court jester, is impeccable; his dirty talk really influenced people. Hoffman was also quite convincing in *All the President's Men* (1976) and John Schlesinger's torturous *Marathon Man* (1976). But then came the troubles at First Artists Productions and the rankling debate over the final cuts of *Straight Time* (1978) and *Agatha* (1978); neither is half so bad as Hoffman asserts. *Kramer vs. Kramer* (1979) showed Hoffman back on stride, as everyone's favorite graduate mellowed into one of the most loving fathers of the decade.

Warren Beatty, best known for his portrayal of Clyde Barrow in *Bonnie and Clyde* (1967), emerged as another sensitive hero in his Seventies performances and proved himself an equally astute filmmaker. Altman's *McCabe and Mrs. Miller* (1971) and Pakula's *The Parallax View* (1974) challenged his artistry considerably more than Richard Brooks' *$$$* (1971), but it was his own participation in *Shampoo* (1975), which he co-scripted, that led to his remarkable production of *Heaven Can Wait* (1978), a remake of *Here Comes Mr. Jordan* (1941) which garnered Beatty more Oscar nominations than anyone except Orson Welles ever received in a single year. *Heaven Can Wait* is no *Citizen Kane,* but producer, co-director, co-screenwriter, and

Dustin Hoffman in Arthur Penn's LITTLE BIG MAN (1970).

Dustin Hoffman in Bob Fosse's LENNY (1974).

star Beatty did create one of the wittiest films of the decade. His Joe Pendleton, a Los Angeles Rams quarterback called to Paradise too soon and resurrected as Leo Farnsworth, a wealthy businessman, drifts through a society rife with competition, greed, and incompetence with just the proper aloofness, the comic perspective, to transform the mundane into the inspired.

The two sensitive surgeons of *M*A*S*H* (1970), Donald Sutherland and Elliott Gould, both had prolific if somewhat undistinguished careers in the Seventies. Sutherland took some roles for a single speech or a single sequence (*Little Murders*, 1971; *National Lampoon Animal House*, 1978), some for their courageous political statements (*Johnny Got His Gun*, 1971; *Steelyard Blues*, 1972), others for the opportunity to work with a distinguished foreign director (*Don't Look Now*, 1973, Nicholas Roeg; *Casanova*, 1976, Federico Fellini; *1900*, 1977, Bernardo Bertolucci), and still others just for the money (*S*P*Y*S*, 1974; *The Eagle Has Landed*, 1977). For all these diverse undertakings, however, he still performed best as the virtuous small-town detective (*Klute*, 1971), the innocent adrift in a decadent society (*The Day of the Locust*, 1975), or the appealing hero trapped in a nightmare of corruption and conformity (*Invasion of the Body Snatchers*, 1978). Unwillingly and unwittingly, Donald Sutherland was most successful as the James Stewart of the Seventies, the mumbling John Doe thrust reluctantly into a society he does not understand and cannot master.

Elliott Gould played an even more vulnerable urban dropout in minor comedies like *Getting Straight* (1970), *Move* (1970), and *I Love My Wife* (1970). Gould was unable to expand on this characterization, however, despite an impressively supportive performance by Diane Keaton in *I Will . . . I Will . . . For Now* (1976), Norman Panama's disappointing satire of adultery and sex therapy, one of the earliest films to get its participants into California's ubiquitous hot tub. Gould tried a couple more films with Donald Sutherland (*Little Murders*, 1971; *S*P*Y*S*, 1974), and did some finely nuanced work for Robert Altman (*The Long Goodbye*, 1973; *California Split*, 1974; *Nashville*, 1975), but his career was in precipitous decline by decade's end. *The Silent Partner*, a low-budget Canadian feature, showed some glimmer of his old vitality, but it could not erase the colossal embarrassment of his escapades with a boxing kangaroo named *Matilda* (1978).

Warren Beatty and James Mason in HEAVEN CAN WAIT (1978).

Elliott Gould, Donald Sutherland, and Bobby Troup in Robert Altman's M*A*S*H (1970).

The most exciting new male stars of Seventies Hollywood—James Caan, Bruce Dern, Jon Voight, Al Pacino, Robert De Niro, and Jack Nicholson—took their craft too seriously to clown with pugilistic marsupials. Caan, for example, turned down a four million dollar offer to play the lead in *Superman* (1978). When Marlon Brando called and asked, "What's the matter, isn't the money enough?" Caan's reply was most revealing, "The money is incredible. But *you* don't have to wear the suit." This new breed of stars considered themselves artists, not artisans; they looked for artistic potential as well as profits.

Artist James Caan had few hits over the decade, but many of his portrayals occur in the most interesting cinema of the period, projects mature in conception and accomplished in execution, like Francis Coppola's thoughtful though flawed American odyssey, *The Rain People* (1969), Jack Smight's neglected interpretation of John Updike's *Rabbit Run* (1970), and the immensely moving telefilm, *Brian's Song* (1971). The same year Caan limned the mercurial Sonny in *The Godfather* (1972), he also worked on *Slither* (1973), director Howard Zieff's auspicious debut. As Dick Kanipsia, Caan is bewildered, frazzled, and disoriented by the zany antics of free spirits Barry Fenaka (Peter Boyle) and Kitty Kopetzky (Sally Kellerman), until a shoot-out at a trailer park bingo game almost undoes them all; Kanipsia's sufferings in the batty world of recreational vehicles kept the film's meager audience in conniptions. In *Cinderella Liberty* (1974), Caan's performance as roustabout sailor John Baggs combined bitter tears and barely contained rage in Mark Rydell's impressive treatment of Darryl Ponicsan's screenplay. *Freebie and the Bean* (1974) gave Caan and Alan Arkin much room for philosophizing between car crashes and bathroom shoot-outs, while *Funny Lady* (1975) proved another jarring encounter between a male star and Barbra Streisand. Karel Reisz's *The Gambler* (1974) afforded Caan his juiciest role, as a City College English professor consumed by his feeling that he can beat any odds. Professor James Toback's screenplay proved too harsh for most tastes, but Caan is unforgettable cadging money from his mother, posturing with loan sharks, or just contemplating his crumbling fortunes immersed in a bathtub. His topsy-turvy romance with the surprisingly effective Laura Hutton counterpoints his final gut-wrenching physical disfigurement by a prostitute. *Rollerball* (1975), Norman Jewison's futuristic satire, adapted from William Harrison's

Diane Keaton and Elliott Gould in Norman Panama's I WILL, I WILL . . . FOR NOW (1975).

James Caan in Karel Reisz's THE GAMBLER (1974).

provocative *Esquire* story, revealed Caan's physical side, though his dialogue with the imperial Bartholomew (John Houseman), the doughty librarian (Ralph Richardson), and the concerned Cletus (Moses Gunn) showed an accomplished actor at ease with his peers. Peckinpah's *The Killer Elite* (1975) and Richard Attenborough's *A Bridge Too Far* (1977) were rather routine adventure films, but Caan brought a good deal of concentration to bear on his Westerns, *Comes a Horseman* (1978) and *Another Man, Another Chance* (1978), a Claude Lelouch film with a photographer's eye for detail and a delicate Gallic sense of romance.

Bruce Dern spent much of the Seventies seeking roles with the proper delicacy so he could escape the "madman" image he feared would smother his career just as it stifled Anthony Perkins after *Psycho* (1960). In an interview with Dick Stelzer published in *The Star Treatment*, a shockingly frank collection of twenty celebrity ruminations on "the inner torment that led them to psychotherapy," a volume indicative of the decade's penchant for candor and gossip, Dern confessed that it was "maddening to have agents and producers say 'Yeah, well, he's maybe the best actor in the business, but he's not Clint Eastwood, and he never will be.' That throws you into a depression more than anything else." The depression was deepened, Dern continued, because "I don't want to be Clint Eastwood. I want to play interesting, multidimensional people in movies that are entertaining. That's all I've ever wanted."

Dern's high standards led to some most daring choices of acting assignments; his performances frequently drew more good critical notices than paying customers. Coach Bullion, for example, was a pivotal player in Jack Nicholson's accomplished but perhaps too Brechtian *Drive, He Said* (1970), and his Lowell and the space freighter Valley Forge are the entire focus in the neglected *Silent Running* (1971). His Jason was really *The King of Marvin Gardens* (1972), just as his "Big Bob" Freelander ruled the stage in *Smile* (1975). For all these fine performances, however, the mass audience frequently saw Dern portray only the kinky, the villainous, and the unbalanced sides of human experience. His career was enmired in the jealous dementia of Tom Buchanan in *The Great Gatsby* (1974), the chilling psychotic bloodlust of Lander in *Black Sunday* (1977), and the cruel compulsive tics of the Detective in Walter Hill's *The Driver* (1978), a film despised

Bruce Dern in Bob Rafelson's THE KING OF MARVIN GARDENS (1972).

domestically but lavishly praised in Europe. Dern seemed married by decade's end to the do or die, "I must be hero" delusions which haunted the disillusioned marine officer who gallops naked into the sea to die in *Coming Home* (1978).

Dern's blond alter ego in *Coming Home*, Jon Voight, faced his own problems choosing roles that were both challenging and commercial. One of his best performances, for example, as "A" in the Kafkaesque foreign feature, *The Revolutionary* (1970), directed by Paul Williams from Hans Koningsberger's complex script, was rarely seen in America; and much of Voight's portrayal of Milo Minderbinder ended on the cutting floor as Mike Nichols tried to streamline his elephantine failure, *Catch 22* (1970). *Deliverance* (1972) was a big hit, but Voight's performance as Ed, the pipe-smoking, seemingly happily married man, suffered from a lack of credibility that haunted many of the conveniently symbolic roles in this poetic allegory. Voight was splendid as a boxer in Charles Eastman's lean parable *The All American Boy* (1973), but it was his undisciplined appearance as Billy in Franco Zeffirelli's sudsy remake *The Champ* (1978) which k.o.'d fans. Neither the liberal good spirits of *Conrack* (1974) nor the dark terror of *The Odessa File* (1974) had garnered much of an audience, so it was Voight's own success in capturing the role of Luke in *Coming Home* (1978) that paved the way to Zeffirelli's immensely popular tear jerker and a renaissance in Voight's career.

For Al Pacino, the Seventies have been a constant upward spiral of fame and achievement. The Bobby of Jerry Schatzberg's *cinéma verité* drug opus, *The Panic in Needle Park* (1971), which profited from the sterling script by Joan Didion and John Gregory Dunne, quickly matured as Michael Corleone of *The Godfather* (1972) and *Godfather II* (1974). No challenge seemed too great for Pacino; undaunted by Brando, he matched stride for stride with Gene Hackman in *Scarecrow* (1973) as they shouted and scratched their way across America in an existential pilgrimage. *Scarecrow* was photographed by Vilmos Zsigmond, and the emotions are so intense and fully realized that the cinematographer's careful echo of the Pieta when Max (Hackman) comforts his battered Leon (Pacino) does not seem overwrought.

Sidney Lumet's direction of *Serpico* (1973) kept all eyes on Pacino as the hirsute and diminutive detective who blew the whistle on corruption in the ranks. Pacino obviously enjoyed the clipped diction, nervous hand movements, and hippie ensemble this role required. Even as Serpico hobbles off to exile in his hooded cape, carrying books he knows can never capture the rugged truths of city streets, Pacino keeps the excitement in his eyes, an intensely focused energy that tears through the screen. *Dog Day Afternoon* (1975), also directed by Lumet, was based on the August 22, 1972, stickup of the Chase Manhattan Bank at Avenue P and Third Street in Brooklyn by "Littlejohn" Wajtowicz; screenwriter Frank R. Pierson transforms this media event into a careful character study of Sonny (Pacino), a married homosexual desperate for acceptance and love. Sonny negotiates cannily with the police, deals compassionately with his hostages, and prances for the large crowd of onlookers, but all the while he is grimly aware of the futility of his grandstanding. As the television blares on about Sonny's love for Leon (Chris Sarandon) and the proposed sex-change operation, Sonny tells his slow-witted partner (a resplendent characterization by John Cazale), "It doesn't matter, Sal. It's only a freak show to them." One bizarre spinoff of *Dog Day Afternoon* was Ray Olsen's 1975 attempt to imitate the film and use hostages in Greenwich Village to free Patty Hearst, the Harrises, and Wendy Yoshimura. Fact had been transmuted by fiction into a new fact.

Pacino's *Bobby Deerfield* (1977), produced and directed by Sydney Pollack, misfired when the romance between the racer and the terminally ill Lillian (Marthe Keller) got lost in the scenery, but Pacino's interludes with Lydia (Anny Duperey) and his exchanges with his brother (Walter McGinn) are very moving. *And Justice for All* (1979), starring Pacino as a young lawyer battling the system, was a return to the *Serpico* mold, and audiences loved it.

Actor Robert De Niro's greatest triumphs were recorded on the streets of New York City, including the *Mean Streets* (1973) of Little Italy, the congested traffic lanes of *Taxi Driver* (1976), the studio reconstructions of Forties *New York, New York* (1977), and the crowded Bronx of *The Raging Bull* (1980). De Niro, a dedicated professional, is almost monomaniacal in his preparations for a role; he actually learned Sicilian for *Godfather II*, where he managed exquisitely to look like a young Brando playing a young Vito Corleone, and he gained over forty pounds to play an over-the-hill Jake La Motta in

Al Pacino in Sidney Lumet's SERPICO (1973).

Robert DeNiro in Francis Coppola's GODFATHER II (1974).

The Raging Bull. No role is without its challenges and accomplishments for this consummate craftsman: De Niro immerses himself so completely in roles that the character possesses him. One minute he is a hillbilly ball player, Bruce Pearson, in *Bang the Drum Slowly* (1973) with a crooked mouth full of chewing tobacco and a head slightly out of line with his shoulders; the next, he is the frowning, intense, formal Monroe Stahr of *The Last Tycoon* (1976). For director Martin Scorsese, he can be a doomed small-time hustler, a demented loner, or even a romantic hipster, while for Bernardo Bertolucci he is the decadent grandson Alfredo of the courtly lord of an Italian manor (Burt Lancaster) in the Marxist epic *1900* (1977). De Niro's ability to submerge himself in a character and his extraordinary range allowed him to be one of the most sought-after talents of the Seventies without becoming a celebrity jet-setter. His talent was considerably greater than his notoriety.

The most celebrated actor of the decade, and one of the most gifted, Jack Nicholson, made few attempts to disguise his personality in a characterization. Nicholson is an old-fashioned star; for all his dedication to a performance, his own ego and energy always bubble through. The philosophical, fun-loving lawyer of *Easy Rider* (1969) has the same ornery streak as Robert Eroica Dupea, the hard-hatted pianist of *Five Easy Pieces* (1970) who knows how to order the toast he wants in a restaurant even if he cannot find inner peace. Wheeling-dealing Jonathan, the sadly impotent promoter of *Carnal Knowledge* (1971), might well have forsaken his penthouse slide show and expensive whorehouse for the desolate Atlantic City and the deserted boardwalk schemer David strolls in *The King of Marvin Gardens* (1971). Boisterous gob Buddusky on his *Last Detail* (1973) seems as world weary and confused as the slow-witted J. J. Gittes of *Chinatown* (1974), a private eye just as scarred by his discovery of corruption and incest as by his eerie mutilation by the symbolic "man with knife," director Roman Polanski. Italian director Michelangelo Antonioni saw Jack Nicholson as the perfect protean identity for his structuralist metafiction *The Passenger* (1974), while Czech director Milos Forman captured Nicholson's anarchic bent beautifully in the Oscar-winning *One Flew Over the Cuckoo's Nest* (1975). As R. P. McMurphy, Nicholson brings echoes of Sixties American International biker movies, of *Easy Rider* and the whole dropout scene, powerfully to bear on Ken

Kesey's classic text. Forman's dramatic switch in point of view from the fog of the novel's narrator, Chief Bromden, to the film's stark war of wills between sports-happy, whoremongering, speed-boating, good-ol'-boy McMurphy and the castrating, manipulative, sternly ascetic Nurse Ratched (Oscar-winner Louise Fletcher) demands that Nicholson win the audience's sympathy quickly, draw them into his imaginary World Series and convince them to applaud his fatal escape from a lobotomized existence.

Given his stunning success in *One Flew Over the Cuckoo's Nest,* audiences demanded too much from Nicholson, and could not see the charms of *The Missouri Breaks* (1976) nor the subtler revelations of *The Last Tycoon* (1976). *Going South* (1978), which Nicholson directed, was an amusing Western romance between hard-working Julia (Mary Steenburgen) and a drifter she marries to save from hanging, Moon (Nicholson), but it suffered from Nicholson's inability to sense when too much of a star's mugging was spoiling a film. The sexy outlaw tries to convince Julia there is more to life than back-breaking labor and an exhausting battle against the Great Southwestern Railroad: he favors the "Mexican" way of life, "slow days and fast nights." Unfortunately, audiences found nothing quite fast enough in this self-indulgent project.

Nicholson the star obviously needed a superstar director to strike the balance between personality and persona, so he turned to an acknowledged cinematic genius famous for his strong control of every facet of a production, Stanley Kubrick, a New Yorker who adopted England as his home. Kubrick's projects tended to be lengthy undertakings, with elaborate plans and meticulous workmanship, but the results were truly sublime. Kubrick virtually reinvented space fantasies with his mind-boggling intellectual puzzle *2001: A Space Odyssey* (1968); then he showed how original literary adaptations could be with his apocalyptically violent *A Clockwork Orange* (1971) and his glacially slow, sensuously ravishing *Barry Lyndon* (1975), a film that future generations will rediscover and proclaim a masterpiece.

Nicholson and Kubrick spent a grueling two years filming Stephen King's *The Shining*. American novelist Diane Johnson, who collaborated on the script, revealed that director Kubrick wanted to make "the best horror film ever made," which he saw as a considerable intellectual challenge: "The film must be plausible, use no cheap

Jack Nicholson in Bob Rafelson's FIVE EASY PIECES (1970).

Karen Black and Jack Nicholson in FIVE EASY PIECES (1970).

tricks, have no holes in the plot and no failure in motivation. It must be a scary horror film without insulting the intelligence of the audience." In preproduction, Kubrick and Johnson spent their evenings watching Jack Nicholson's earlier movies. Nicholson was the key to their film, they well knew, and they were ecstatic to discover he was best in active and voluble roles, for their basic concept of their protagonist was that of "a driven and energetic" person. Nicholson seemed the right actor for the right part in *The Shining*. Carl Laemmle would have approved.

5. I Am Woman

It isn't what I do, but how I do it. It isn't what I say, but how I say it. And how I look when I do it and say it.
MAE WEST

WILLIAM GOLDMAN'S best seller, *Tinsel*, promoted as "*the* Hollywood Novel," has as its central concern the casting of a sex goddess to play an aging Marilyn Monroe type contemplating her own suicide as she wanders nude through her apartment recalling her lovers. After tracing the lives and troubles of some likely candidates for this explicitly erotic stardom, the novel concludes with the worldly wise producer, Julian Garvey, making a deal with agents representing Barbra Streisand. His inexperienced son, Noel, is shocked that Julian could ever see Streisand as a sex symbol, but Julian quickly explains: ". . . we're changing things around here and there to fit her talents. There will be no nudity anymore. She will be beautifully and tastefully dressed in lingerie throughout the last hour of the picture. She will not be a fading sex star, she will be a fading singing star—" Streisand is interested, it seems, because she will be on screen alone for an hour, wandering through rooms where her music plays. Julian, on the other hand, exults in an anticipated eleven million dollar profit. He has, after all, signed the biggest star in the world, "the only star . . . who's a star everywhere—records-clubs-TV-films—no one else is close."

No other film star has, as *Cue* critic George Haddad-Garcia observed in his perceptive tribute "The Lady Is a Champ" (July 6, 1979), "so completely dominated a decade as Streisand has the Seventies, even though she has made relatively few movies. . . ." Streisand is the reigning box-office champ. Everything she touches turns to gold or platinum. She faces no problems of sexual identity or of proper characterizations for a woman in an age of liberation; Streisand is, first and foremost, an entertainer.

This tough little Jewish girl from New York got her start in films playing another rugged big-city trouper, Fanny Brice, in William Wyler's energetic adaptation of Isobel Lennart's play, *Funny Girl*

Barbra Streisand.

(1968). The Broadway transplant, *Hello Dolly* (1969), was next, with dapper Gene Kelly directing Barbra as an under-age Dolly Levi; then came Vincente Minelli's unfortunate vision of *On a Clear Day You Can See Forever* (1970), with clairvoyant Daisy Gamble (Streisand) hypnotized by Dr. Marc Chabot (Yves Montand). Streisand tried to break the musical mold, playing the daffy prostitute Delores opposite a moustached George Segal in director Herbert Ross's antic comedy *The Owl and the Pussycat* (1971). Strikingly outfitted in leather boots, miniskirt, and patterned stockings, wrapped casually in a terrycloth robe, and even fleetingly and discreetly naked in the bathtub with would-be writer Felix, Streisand turns the milquetoast who reported her nocturnal activities to the landlord into a lover, who boldly flings his typewriter away for romance.

Streisand works the same kind of transformation on the stuffy musicologist Howard Bannister (Ryan O'Neal) in Peter Bogdanovich's highly derivative *What's Up Doc?* (1972), a pale imitation of Howard Hawks's classic *Bringing Up Baby*. As Judy Maxwell, Streisand is a one-person wrecking crew, foiling crimes, disrupting banquets, and running down pedestrians with a delivery cart. Unfortunately, the script by noted Hollywood scribes Buck Henry, Robert Benton, and David Newman is long on chases and confusion and short on credibility and coherence.

Up the Sandbox (1972) also has script problems, though the screenplay is by Paul Zindel, based on the pro-motherhood novel by Anne Roiphe, the author of *Digging Out* and *Long Division*. This Walter Mitty-like comic reverie features Streisand as frustrated housewife Margaret Reynolds, whose fantasy lives include those of a journalist interviewing Fidel Castro and a captive held by an Amazon tribe. From a feminist perspective, this is one of Streisand's most troubling roles. Joan Mellen noted in her provocative text, *Women and Their Sexuality in the New Film,* that *Up the Sandbox* seems to have as "its central objective, the conclusive demonstration of the hollowness of the advocacy of the women's movement." The frustrations Margaret confronts at home never seem quite so bad as the insanities within the revolutionary movements; the sandbox is clearly preferable to, for example, that "goddamned dyke," the transvestite Fidel Castro of her dreams.

144

Barbra Streisand and Jacobo Morales in Irvin Kershner's UP THE SANDBOX (1972).

145

The Way We Were (1973) also mangles some important political themes as it develops the improbable romance of a left-wing Jewish ugly duckling, Katie, and the biggest man on campus, the apolitical literate WASP Hubbell (Robert Redford). Their love story spans three decades, a world war, the Hollywood Ten trial, and their divorce. Streisand has some splendid moments miming Harpo Marx in a comedy skit, but mostly *The Way We Were* is a Marvin Hamlisch score, Streisand's overwrought theme song, and Redford's beaming smile. Where producer Ray Stark might have explored the crisis of conscience which haunted show business in the Fifties, he contents himself with ineffectual equivocation. Obviously, all eyes were on the box office, where tearjerkers do much better than treatises.

For Pete's Sake (1974) marks Streisand's return to madcap comedy, though the laughs are rather forced in director Peter Yates's all too mechanical farce. Improbably cast as "Henry," opposite husband Peter (Michael Sarrazin), Streisand schemes zanily to repay her huge debts. The resultant escapades involve bizarre disguises, a wild ride on an ill-tempered bull, and some wacky adventures above and below street level. None of these frolics, however, make up for the basic lack of invention and originality in this witless film. Streisand followed this lackluster comedy with an equally predictable sequel to *Funny Girl, Funny Lady* (1975), the further exploits of Fanny Brice, focusing on the years she was married to Billy Rose (James Caan). Fortunately, this trite biography had plenty of high-stepping production numbers expertly filmed by director Herbert Ross, some masterful Technicolor photography by James Wong Howe, and a wondrously articulated performance by America's superstar chanteuse.

A Star Is Born (1976) was Barbra Streisand's attempt to go Judy Garland one better, with aspiring songstress Esther Hoffman wooing John Norman Howard (Kris Kristofferson), an alcoholic has-been. As in so many remakes, however, the concept was considerably better than the execution, and the convoluted interactions of the producer, ex-hairdresser Jon Peters, the executive producer, Barbra Streisand, and the "gossip must out" screenwriters Joan Didion, John Gregory Dunne, and Frank Pierson (who also directed) made the *New Yorker* reaction to the original David O. Selznick dramatic version seem preternaturally apt; the new *Star Is Born* was, to borrow the magazine's old description, "a peculiar sort of masochistic, self-congratulatory Hollywood orgy."

146

Barbra Streisand and Robert Redford in Sydney Pollack's THE WAY WE WERE (1973).

Streisand's next feature, *The Main Event* (1979), was her attempt to go Sylvester Stallone one round further in a comic version of *Rocky,* with a hip Jewish Princess transforming a pretty-faced loafer (Ryan O'Neal) into a championship contender. The film cost only seven million dollars to make, but Warner Brothers committed over eight million dollars to the advertising campaign in an attempt to knock out the summer competition. Much of the humor in *The Main Event* is vulgar, leering, sexist, racist, locker-room bawdy. There are few jabs in the film; it is as though everyone in the production was so afraid of the audience that they felt they had to throw roundhouse rights all the time, emphasizing, for example, Streisand's shock at male nudity and locking the cosmetics queen in a cabin full of lecherous blacks and Hispanics. The whole film is clumsy shadow boxing, with nothing resembling championship style, yet fans still clamored to see Streisand, who put much of her posterior on display in posters for *The Main Event.* Her co-star, Ryan O'Neal, was quite cynical about his second romantic film with Streisand, and spent much of his time in promotional interviews mocking his dangerous sparring partner: "That Streisand can hurt you. She's a sneaky puncher and in the clinch she sings in your ear."

O'Neal, whose own popularity was plummeting, did offer, however, some fine insights into Streisand and her career when he discussed her next project, a musical based on an Isaac B. Singer story: "If audiences are sick of seeing Barbra Streisand playing Barbra Streisand, then wait till they see her as *Yentl, the Yeshiva Girl.* They'll want her to go back to being Barbra Streisand." Robert Stigwood also approached Barbra Streisand about playing the lead in *Evita,* the smash-hit musical staged in London by Harold Prince and composers Tim Rice and Andrew Lloyds-Webber. Streisand wanted over three million dollars in advance and a large percentage before she would play the South American seductress-patriot-saint, Eva Peron, whose flamboyant life had already inspired Radley Metzger's kinky nudie, *Little Mother* (1973).

The flood of low-budget nudies and pornographic loops made it hard for Hollywood sex queens to compete in the Seventies. "Tits and ass" seemed too tame for the modern temperament; maintaining the old erotic tension in an age when so many took it all off was a considerable challenge. Perhaps the most successful "no show" sexpot of the decade was the statuesque Raquel Welch, whose refusal to disrobe on screen did as much for her career as did her awe-inspiring décolletage. Welch's pneumatic breasts jiggled suggestively through many of the worst films of the decade, including Michael Sarne's inept variations on Gore Vidal's novel *Myra Breckinridge* (1970), an avant-garde ode to bad taste; Joseph McGrath's muddled misinterpretation of Terry Southern's novel *The Magic Christian* (1970), a commercial spoof that proved unsalable; and Edward Dmytryk's clumsy, voyeuristic version of *Bluebeard* (1972), an inartistic and pretentious abuse of Richard Burton's amorous talents.

Raquel Welch seemed always about-to-be but never quite nude in a sad assortment of failed genre exercises. Her Seventies Western, for example, *Hannie Caulder* (1971), featured her draped in a blanket, flashing her thighs through a raunchy narrative of rape and bloody revenge; her sports movie, *Kansas City Bomber* (1972), did as much for Spandex bras as it did for Ace bandages. As Detective Eileen McHenry, Welch was the butt of all the jokes in the Burt Reynolds caper film *Fuzz* (1972). Then she filled out the scooped-neck costumes in Richard Lester's period pieces, *The Three Musketeers* (1973) and *The Four Musketeers* (1974), and in Richard Fleischer's all-star version of *The Prince and the Pauper*, entitled *Crossed Swords* (1977); Welch managed to bring some slinky sexuality to James Ivory's otherwise tepid *Wild Party* (1974) in a mind-boggling gown by Ralph Lauren. Most of the decade Raquel Welch was there to provide wide-eyed sex appeal. No role summarizes her achievement more clearly than her portrayal of a flustered ambulance attendant in *Mother, Jugs, and Speed* (1976) in this trio, Bill Cosby is Mother and Harvey Keitel is Speed.

British-born sexpot Jacqueline Bisset stripped to the waist in *The Grasshopper* (1969) to show a producer getting a haircut that she had the jugs necessary to make it as a Las Vegas showgirl, bragging as she peeled that her "tickets" were the envy of her neighborhood. Years later in *The Deep* (1977) her braless wet tee-shirt aquatics would titillate audiences and fill billboards across America; Bisset's undeniable sex appeal even prompted distributors to resurrect the best forgotten psychodrama *Secrets* (1971), which features a youthful Bisset in a nude scene. Most of the decade, however, Bisset tried to broaden her range, deemphasizing beauty and stressing instead her

149

Raquel Welch in James Ivory's THE WILD PARTY (1974).

Jacqueline Bisset in Peter Yates' THE DEEP (1977).

dramatic gifts. Her most successful ventures were François Truffaut's delightful homage to movies, *Day for Night* (1973), and Sidney Lumet's star-studded, slightly overinflated dramatization of Agatha Christie's *Murder on the Orient Express* (1974). Her later outings in the *roman à clef* tabloid biography *The Greek Tycoon* (1978) and in the byzantine gastronomic travelogue *Who Is Killing the Great Chefs of Europe?* (1978) proved less delectable, so Jacqueline Bisset's hopes of escaping the sex-goddess syndrome rest on her future work.

Buxom television celebrity Farrah Fawcett turned to film to escape "The Farrah Phenomenon" and *Charlie's Angels,* as Americans gobbled up two million copies of her subliminally seductive poster (which in a startling confirmation of Professor Wilson Bryan Key's revealing thesis rather boldly outlined the word "sex" in Farrah's luxurious tresses), bought tons of the cosmetics she endorsed, and rushed to beauty parlors to imitate her hairstyle. Farrah Fawcett's film projects, however, proved remarkably like the pap which suffices for television broadcast. *Somebody Killed Her Husband* (1978) was a routine romantic gothic, with papier mâché monsters providing a colorful conclusion to a trite plot. *Sunburn* (1979) was, as *Variety* so aptly punned, "no scorcher"; only Farrah Fawcett's open-to-the-navel wetsuit gave any bounce to this hackneyed insurance fraud comedy. Both these features were destined for quick sale to television networks, and Farrah Fawcett ended the decade doing special "guest appearances" on *Charlie's Angels.*

Goldie Hawn was one of the few women able to move from television to the big screen, and her success depended largely on her comedic talents. Women were more easily assimilated in Seventies movies if they could sing (Barbra Streisand), dance (Leslie Brown), or handle jokes (Sally Field, Diane Keaton). Audience praise for liberated characterizations usually came much more slowly than applause for frivolous entertainment.

Goldie Hawn was the decade's lovable "dumb blonde," splashing around merrily with Peter Sellers in *There's a Girl in My Soup* (1970), snuggling and smuggling with Warren Beatty in *$$$* (1971), and breaking both convention and hearts as the buoyant Jill in *Butterflies Are Free* (1972). Director Steven Spielberg envisioned the character Lou Jean as "the real villain . . . the heavy" of *Sugarland Express* (1974), but audiences cheered Hawn's gritty vagrant and not the police. Only

Goldie Hawn in Colin Higgins' FOUL PLAY (1978).

Goldie Hawn and Warren Beatty in Hal Ashby's SHAMPOO (1975).

The Girl from Petrovka (1974) proved a misadventure for Hawn; the gorgeous photography of Vilmos Zsigmond could not conceal the ill-advised accents, the vapid romance, or the failed seriousness of this epic clinker. Goldie Hawn left the role of the Russian Oktyabrina far behind, however, returning as the zany miniskirted Jill of Hal Ashby's *Shampoo*, one of her most touchingly hysterical performances. *The Duchess and Dirtwater Fox* (1978) was an ill-conceived showcase for the talents of George Segal, but *Foul Play* (1978) made Goldie Hawn the center of the cyclone in Colin Higgins' whirlwind summer hit. Warned to "beware the dwarf," librarian Gloria Munz (Goldie Hawn) is catapulted into a world of wild chases, assassination plots, and unexpected dangers. Surrounded by pearl-handled daggers, black limousines, and albino villains, this contemporary little girl lost depends on a doddering landlord (Burgess Meredith) with a pet python with the Salingeresque name Esme and on a trusting policeman (Chevy Chase); she also constantly foils the best-laid plans of a foppish would-be playboy (Dudley Moore), a libertine whose erotic devices ensnare him far more often than his prey. In *Foul Play,* the light opera of *The Mikado* fittingly counterpoints an exotic plot to kill the Pope. As the curtain goes down on the operetta, the climactic chase, and the comedy, Goldie Hawn and Chevy Chase kiss; both these refugees from innovative television comedies (*Saturday Night Live, Laugh In*) have enough show-biz sense to embrace the most tried and true cliché of romantic chases, the final joyous physical affirmation that, even in Seventies Hollywood, love and romance conquer all.

Television's giggling "Gidget," Sally Field, who also played the winsome "Flying Nun," made her leap to movies in the very conventional Western, *The Way West* (1967). After a long hiatus, Sally Field returned to cinema in Bob Rafelson's disappointing assessment of body building and the New South, *Stay Hungry* (1976), where she seemed almost as tongue-tied as the muscle-bound Arnold Schwarzenegger. Fortunately, her romance with Burt Reynolds blossomed at the same time he made his biggest hit, *Smokey and the Bandit* (1977), in which she co-starred. Sally Field had demonstrated how well she could act when given the chance in the television version of *Sybil,* yet she was the first to admit she "would have had trouble paying the bills" if Reynolds had not cast her in his comic adventures, *The End*

(1978) and *Hooper* (1978). *Heroes* (1977), television personality Henry Winkler's cinematic debut, stuck Sally Field with all the bad checks, and *Beyond the Poseidon Adventure* (1978) was a major embarrassment for all aboard. Even the scenery seemed to blush when a blind man joined the bedraggled climb to freedom. Sally Field ended the decade, however, in an extraordinarily fine "little picture," *Norma Rae* (1979), an offbeat and affecting study of union organizing in Southern textile mills and of one woman's discovery of her own personal worth. Norma Rae has been in many cheap hotel rooms and has lost one husband to drinking and feuding, yet she manages to maintain enough innocence and enthusiasm to lead her co-workers in their efforts to organize. Norma Rae proved such a "sumptuous" human portrayal that it merited the cherubic Field the "best actress" award at Cannes and the Oscar and assured she would never have to play second fiddle again.

Madeline Kahn made a career of co-starring in the Seventies, anchoring some of the great comedies of the decade. Working with Peter Bogdanovich, she managed some fine pratfalls in *What's Up Doc?* (1972), gave a much-needed lift to *Paper Moon* (1973), and even preserved a modicum of dignity in his debacle, *At Long Last Love* (1975). For Robert Moore, she managed to make a tired Neil Simon routine about aliases seem much better than it was in *The Cheap Detective* (1978), just as she helped Gene Wilder milk some lame burlesque for chuckles in *The Adventures of Sherlock Holmes's Smarter Brother* (1975).

Madeline Kahn's real comrade, however, is Mel Brooks; she is the most accomplished farceur in many of his witty genre exercises. As Lili Von Shtupp, the showgirl heartbreaker of *Blazing Saddles* (1974), she discombobulates the black sheriff with a big sausage and brings the saloon down with her earthy lyrics and black lace lingerie. In *Young Frankenstein* (1974) she is the pristine Elizabeth, elegantly clad in a jeweled turban and wrapped in expensive furs, but soon discomfited by the strange machinations at the castle. In *High Anxiety* (1978), Kahn plays Victoria Brisbane, whose quest for a lost relative further complicates the psycho-comedy. Playing it straight or strictly for laughs, Madeline Kahn has a wondrously elastic face, capable of assaying violent surprise in the twitch of a muscle, the rapid movement of an eye, or a suppressed cough.

156

If Madeline Kahn found her mentor in Mel Brooks, Diane Keaton's Svengali is her one-time lover, now friend, Woody Allen. Keaton appeared in many fine dramatic roles over the decade, including the pivotal characterization of Kay in *The Godfather* saga (1972; 1974) and the harrowingly physical portrayal of Theresa Dunn in Richard Brooks's violent *Looking for Mr. Goodbar,* a part that she almost rejected because it demanded so much nudity and such intense psychic probing of despair and loneliness. Yet the roles Diane Keaton will be remembered for are all in Woody Allen films.

Diane Keaton seems Allen's alter ego, the small-town Midwestern girl now just as confused by and enamored of New York City as Allen, with his persona of a lovably demented Jewish schmuck from Coney Island. The Keaton-Allen romance began in Herbert Ross's adaptation of Allen's Broadway comedy, *Play It Again, Sam* (1972), an affectionate tribute to *Casablanca,* which features a hirsute film critic Allan (Woody Allen) courting the lovely Linda (Diane Keaton) under the tutelage of a trench coat-clad Bogie. Needless to say, Allan and Linda, themselves in trench coats, enact a memorable scene at a foggy airport runway at night. Keaton remains the romantic interest in *Sleeper* (1973), a science-fiction fantasy; her character Luna's futuristic ideas on sexuality and pleasure deflate a number of romantic notions held by Miles Monroe (Woody Allen).

Love and Death (1975) puts Boris (Woody Allen) and Sonja (Diane Keaton) in bed together in an amusing send-up of Russian novels, replete with conventions for village idiots, slapstick military drills, melodramatic duels, and Allen's hilarious philosophizing on big questions. The Academy Award-winning *Annie Hall* (1977) was Allen's valentine to "old times," Gotham City, and Diane Keaton, whose real family name just happens to be Hall. The film's priceless vignettes about the difficulties in chitchatting with strangers, the awkward moments in family visits, and the frequent breakdowns in communication and failures in intimacy, its reminiscences about the palpable horrors of growing up in Brooklyn, and its comic encounters with lobsters in the kitchen or spiders in the bathroom, all seem like snapshots from Allen and Keaton's own romance. Her acting style is natural, unaffected, and totally engaging. She makes the audience love her multilayered anti-fashions, her gangly awkward posture, and the compulsive nervous tic in her conversation. Annie emerges as the

Diane Keaton in Richard Brooks' LOOKING FOR MR. GOODBAR (1977).

Diane Keaton in Woody Allen's ANNIE HALL (1977).

159

very girl who could appreciate not only *Face to Face* and *The Sorrow and the Pity*, but also the Brooklyn Bridge.

Interiors (1978), Allen's plodding, self-conscious attempt to imitate Ingmar Bergman and Michelangelo Antonioni, is almost unbearably claustrophobic, pessimistic, despairing, and boring, and Diane Keaton has all the worst lines about the embarrassment of "the intimacy of death." Fortunately, *Manhattan* (1979) witnessed a return to form for both Keaton and Allen in a dazzling feature Andrew Sarris proclaimed "the only truly great American film of the Seventies," a masterpiece that "has become a film for the ages by not seeking to be a film for the moment." Keaton's performance as Mary Wilk captures all the depression and elation of the schizophrenic dating scene in New York. Mary Wilk is always torn, caught in the middle, never wholly free. She is a woman writing reviews of Tolstoy's letters at the same time as she struggles to earn some tainted money novelizing a screenplay; her relationship with Isaac Davis (Woody Allen) is at the center of two triangles, one involving his teen-age lover (Mariel Hemingway), and the other his best friend, Mary's boyfriend (Michael Murphy). Keaton eases her way through this complex role with a delicate mix of insouciance and hysteria, sometimes behaving like a condescending twit, yet often revealing a more vulnerable and simpatico personality.

For a good part of the Seventies, foreign actresses dominated American soundstages and screens, monopolizing the major dramatic roles. Glenda Jackson, the leading example of this artistic hegemony, won the Oscar for best actress in 1970 for *Women in Love* and again in 1973 for *A Touch of Class*. Maggie Smith won in 1969 for *The Prime of Miss Jean Brodie,* and films in the early part of the decade allowed little doubt that a major foreign invasion was underway, capitalizing on a public desire for adult fare.

Some stuffy New York critics might complain about the too-frequent display of Glenda Jackson's bare breasts, but she was one of the most prolific and adventuresome talents of the decade. Her range was awesome, spanning the classical repertory (Trevor Nunn's *Hedda* [*Gabler*], 1976; Christopher Miles's *The Maids*, 1975) light comedy (Melvin Frank's *A Touch of Class,* 1973; *Lost and Found,* 1979), soapy biographies (*Mary Queen of Scots,* 1971; *The Incredible Sarah,* 1976), and routine women's pictures (*The Romantic Englishwoman,*

160

*Glenda Jackson and George Segal in Melvin Frank's A TOUCH OF
CLASS (1973).*

1975; *The Class of Miss MacMichael*, 1978). Yet Jackson's best pictures were her daring choices, her energetic characterizations in Ken Russell's extravaganzas, *Women in Love* (1969), *The Music Lovers* (1970), and *The Boy Friend* (1971), and her studied understatement in John Schlesinger's startling *Sunday Bloody Sunday* (1971), a Seventies *mènage à trois* skillfully scripted by critic Penelope Gilliatt and featuring a rich performance by a graying Peter Finch.

Jackson proved her mettle as comedian in the riotous *House Calls* (1978), where her broken jaw mends in time to both chasten and captivate the hospital's most eligible male, a wisecracking surgeon (Walter Matthau). *Nasty Habits* (1977), based on Muriel Spark's delicious Watergate spoof *The Abbess of Crewe*, transposes Washington wiretapping to a bugged cloister where the irrepressible Sister Alexandra (Glenda Jackson) schemes with the Dean-like Sister Winifred (Sandy Dennis) to remain as head of the nunnery. As Mother Superior, Jackson offers an arch characterization, replacing Spark's subtle ironies with rather saucy humor. The film's sacrilegious spoofing still proved too arcane for most audiences; a gaggle of nuns did not seem an apt vehicle for veiled political satire.

Outspoken political opinions often marked the career of Jackson's compatriot Vanessa Redgrave, a British firebrand who used an acceptance speech for her 1977 best actress Oscar to denounce "Zionist hoodlums." No one could assail, however, the talents of this scion of one of England's most gifted acting families. Her portrayal of modern dancer Isadora Duncan in Karel Reisz's *Isadora* (1968), even in its ill-advised American reediting (a butchery that totally ignored the fact that director Reisz had written the standard textbook on film editing), was a gargantuan achievement; the restored American television broadcast version, a considerably longer version, proved there was nuance and substance as well as spectacle in this demonstrative biography. Ken Russell's demonic exploration of sexual repression in a nunnery, *The Devils* (1971), based on Aldous Huxley's *The Devils of Loudun*, was severely edited by censors virtually everywhere it was exhibited, but it proved another major showcase for Redgrave's powerful histrionics.

Vanessa Redgrave demonstrated her considerable theatrical skills in a brooding rendition of *The Seagull* (1968), a reverential version of

Jane Fonda and Vanessa Redgrave in Fred Zinnemann's JULIA (1977).

The Trojan Women (1971), and the verbose biography of *Mary, Queen of Scots* (1971); then she tested her commercial potential in *Murder on the Orient Express* (1974) and the unjustly neglected Sherlock Holmes meets Freud caper, *The Seven Per Cent Solution* (1976). Fred Zinnemann's *Julia* (1977) provided her major role in the decade, opposite Jane Fonda as Lillian Hellman. Rising to the challenge of working with America's finest actress, Vanessa Redgrave transformed the shadowy role of a little rich girl who renounces her cold crystal palace for the white-hot energy of the underground crusade against fascism into a glowing portrait of courage and understanding, everyone's Oscar choice in 1977.

British star Julie Christie's career has been less marked by controversy; slowly but surely, she built on her successes in *Doctor Zhivago* (1965) and *Petulia* (1968) to remain an important presence on American screens. Christie has the knack of finding interesting projects with talented directors; while short, her credits are uniquely distinguished. In 1971, for example, Christie played Marian (Lady Trimingham) in Joseph Losey's hauntingly beautiful *The Go-Between*, Harold Pinter's meticulous adaptation of L. P. Hartley's novel, a big picture on a small theme, which trusted little details to make large revelations. The same year, Christie worked with Warren Beatty in Robert Altman's *McCabe and Mrs. Miller*, another small film with massive appeal for sophisticated audiences. After *Don't Look Now* (1973), Nicholas Roeg's brilliant expansion of an undistinguished story by Daphne Du Maurier, Julie Christie worked for Hal Ashby on *Shampoo* (1975), where she has the most powerful lines, did a cameo in *Nashville* (1975), and made her one blunder of the decade, *Demon Seed* (1977), a bizarre rape fantasy that must have looked better on paper than it does on screen. In 1978, Julie Christie again played opposite Warren Beatty in the highly praised *Heaven Can Wait*, where soft focus photography did much to heighten her romantic appeal. Gossip columnists reported her "at liberty" for the last two years of the decade, moaning the lack of scripts for older women.

Years slide by especially quickly for women in films; yesterday's beauty queen can soon find herself without admirers and roles or recycled as an overweight hussy, a dowager queen, or a psychotic ax-murderess. In less than ten years, for example, Ali MacGraw went

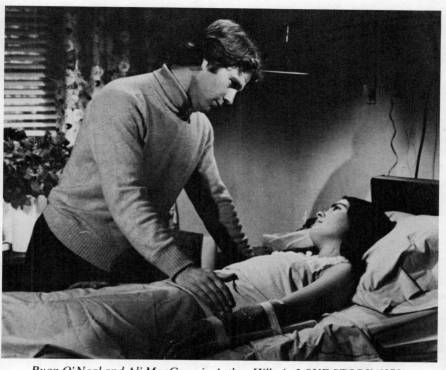

Ryan O'Neal and Ali MacGraw in Arthur Hiller's LOVE STORY (1970).

from the role of everyone's collegiate sweetheart (*Goodbye Columbus*, 1969) to the part of an amoral "older woman" seducing a young athlete (*Players*, 1979). The virginal Cinderella of the epoch's leading tearjerker, *Love Story* (1970), metamorphosed in just ten years into a burnt-out case, the shell-shocked journalist in Peckinpah's *Convoy* (1978). Unable to join Steve McQueen anymore in picaresque adventures like *The Getaway* (1972), Ali MacGraw ended the decade playing in Sidney Lumet's typically New York comedy *Just Tell Me What You Want*, written by Jay Presson Allen. The role was a revelation, Miss MacGraw told interviewers, because the characterization of a pampered mistress who has to realize she cannot blame the man in her life (Alan King) for her own lack of growth "made so much sense to me in terms of my own life. There is a terror of being rejected, the feeling that if I did show people who I really was, they'd decide I wasn't worth loving."

Tuesday Weld's career in the Seventies also illustrates this "young girl/older woman" dichotomy at work. Promising performances in Noel Black's cult classic *Pretty Poison* (1969), Henry Jaglom's enigmatic puzzle *A Safe Place* (1971), and Frank Perry's murky pseudo-happening *Play It As It Lays* (1972) led nowhere. It was a full five years later that this underrated performer returned to the screen as the debauched sister in *Looking for Mr. Goodbar* (1977), a stunning portrayal of a woman who wakes up in the middle of a rather tiresome orgy to discover hers is just one of the many anonymous "naked asses." Two years later, Tuesday Weld joined Nick Nolte in *Who'll Stop the Rain?* (1979). Weld's character emerges as a horrifying zombie, a Dilaudid freak, popping pills mindlessly, while Nolte plays a Nietzschean man tripping along on a samurai fantasy. Weld is a revelation as the deceptively innocent-looking wife, displaced in a disorienting environment, vanquishing her fears and guilt with a quick fix; she is the very image of an America which has brought the war home, an America coming of age without grace or wisdom.

Many of the finest female performers in Seventies films tried to cope with aging by seeking more realistic roles, characterizations outside the panorama of stereotypes Molly Haskell lamented in her well-written survey *From Reverence to Rape*. Hollywood's concept of what "little girls" were made of in the Sixties and early Seventies, Haskell observed, included a demeaning collection of warped per-

Tuesday Weld and Jack Nicholson in Henry Jaglom's A SAFE PLACE (1971).

167

sonalities: "Whores, quasi-whores, jilted mistresses, emotional cripples, drunks, daffy ingenues, Lolitas, kooks, sex-starved spinsters, psychotics, icebergs, zombies, and ballbreakers." Powerful Hollywood women like Shirley MacLaine, Anne Bancroft, Ellen Burstyn, Faye Dunaway, and Jane Fonda were to change all this, as they labored to raise the consciousness of all America.

The Turning Point (1977), featuring both MacLaine and Bancroft, suggests how seriously the homemaker versus professional woman dilemma challenged traditional familial patterns in America. Two years earlier, MacLaine had offered *The Other Half of the Sky: A China Memoir* (1975), an independent exploration of the revolutionary changes in mainland China, evidencing the transformation in the foreign policy of both the United States and China, but *The Turning Point* proved to be the real treatise on revolution, dramatizing the domestic transformation sweeping America. Its spilled drinks and impassioned hair pulling were excellent objective correlatives of the cataclysmic changes being wrought in a country where the majority of married women also held jobs, and where the divorce rate was soaring.

Anne Bancroft, the aging ballerina in *The Turning Point*, also played the lawyer in *Lipstick* (1976), Lamont Johnson's sensationalized study of a rape, the ensuing trial, and its psychological repercussions. Scheduled as a showcase for the body and other talents of Margaux Hemingway (Ernest Hemingway's granddaughter), *Lipstick* actually afforded the biggest break to younger sister Mariel Hemingway, whose childish grief, high-pitched voice, and nervous lip biting proved quite convincing. For all its weaknesses, *Lipstick* provides a potent platform for Anne Bancroft as feminist lawyer Carla Bondi. Her harangue against the blatant defense attempt to malign her client, the fashion-model victim, on the basis of her work and previous sexual experience echoes convincingly the most telling objections activists raise to archaic rape statutes. By the end of the film, audiences actually cheered when Chris McCormick (Margaux Hemingway), incensed at the molestation of her sister Kathy (Mariel Hemingway), pumped repeated shots into the groin of the schoolteacher pervert Gordon Stuart (Chris Sarandon).

Most of Ellen Burstyn's performances involved less visceral thrills, but they stand as hallmarks in a decade when women regained their

168

prominence on screen. Burstyn worked with Paul Mazursky on the ill-fated *Alex in Wonderland* (1970), but her real break came in Peter Bogdanovich's *The Last Picture Show* (1971), where her performance as Lois Farrow, the hard-bitten, no-nonsense mother of blonde beauty Jacy (Cybill Shepherd), garnered the kind of notices that fill an actress's mail box with scripts and keep her agent's phone ringing. Bob Rafelson cast Burstyn opposite Jack Nicholson and Bruce Dern in *The King of Marvin Gardens* (1972), but her good performance went largely for naught as the film sank from view. *The Exorcist* (1973) afforded maximum visibility, and it is a good measure of Ellen Burstyn's professional integrity to note that even in a starring role clearly overshadowed by side-show horrors, she works hard to establish the discordant elements in a working mother's relationship with her troublesome daughter Regan (Linda Blair). Burstyn labors equally strenuously to turn her cameo as Shirley into one of the best sequences of *Harry and Tonto* (1974), an honest evocation of the agreement to disagree which characterizes many father-daughter relationships in an age of changing social mores.

Ellen Burstyn was, Martin Scorsese freely admits and sometimes laments, the real power behind *Alice Doesn't Live Here Anymore* (1974); her participation allowed him to make his "Douglas Sirk type" film with a mainly female crew. Burstyn won the Oscar for her performance as Alice Hyatt, a woman thrown back on her own resources, only to see her dreams of stardom as a singer yield to the grim reality of slinging hash as a waitress in a two-bit cafe. Some of the most powerful moments in the film come when Alice and Flo (Diane Ladd) console each other in a forlorn parking lot. Flo, an embodiment of the life force, tells Alice that the very worst fate of all is "Not doing something you really wanna do," as Alice complains there are "all these . . . options, and I don't know which one to grab for." Some feminists lambasted Alice's final decision to stake her future on the compassionate David (Kris Kristofferson), but few could deny that Ellen Burstyn had created a complex and compelling female character, an historically important portrayal in an era when so many films seemed to view only men's fates as interesting. Ellen Burstyn's later roles in the Seventies were less earthshaking though no less accomplished. In 1977, she worked with the doyen of intellectual cinema, Alain Resnais, on *Providence,* an intense jigsaw puzzle

Ellen Burstyn and Kris Kristofferson in Martin Scorsese's ALICE DOESN'T LIVE HERE ANYMORE (1974).

mingling artistic illusion and inescapable reality; with Jules Dassin on *A Dream of Passion* (1978), a more highly lauded though less successful assessment of similar themes, refracted through a performance of *Medea* starring Melina Mercouri; and with Robert Mulligan on *Same Time Next Year* (1978), a Broadway smash that did not profit from being "opened up" for the screen. Burstyn ended the decade working on Daniel Petrie's *Resurrection*, based on a Lewis John Carlino screenplay about a woman who discovers she has the power to heal.

Former model Faye Dunaway won her Oscar for best actress as the ambitious executive, Diana Christensen, in Sidney Lumet's adaptation of Paddy Chayevsky's *Network* (1976), a chilling portrait of Sammy Glick resurrected after a sex change in television land. Diana hides the lowest of motives behind the high fashions of man-tailored clothes; Dunaway's stylish cool demeanor in this role almost freezes the screen. Her one other good role in the Seventies, as Evelyn Mulwray in Roman Polanski's shimmering descent into the mysteries of *Chinatown*, similarly hinges on her ability to suggest a massive iceberg while displaying only its smallest peaks, wrapping them in soft textures, silken blouses, and velour jackets.

Too many of Dunaway's Seventies roles ignored her skills and emphasized her stylish looks. Dunaway could have profited from a few more roles in period pieces like *Oklahoma Crude* (1973), *Doc*, (1971), or the *Musketeer* sagas (1973 and 1974). Too often she was just a mannequin in films like *The Towering Inferno* (1974), *Voyage of the Damned* (1976), or *The Champ* (1979); even in *Eyes of Laura Mars* (1978), where her character dominates the action, a lot of the best footage depends on her fashions or those of her models. Tied to this ultra-urbane image, Dunaway found it more and more difficult to find roles late in the decade as her waistline expanded; her ability to deal seemed sadly tied to a chic lean and hungry look.

For much of the Seventies, America's most gifted actress, the newest Garbo, had her own image problems. Her outspoken criticism of the war effort and of racism made her the *bête noire* of reactionary forces who tried every sort of harassment and boycott to keep her from working in Hollywood. Her exceptional performance in *They Shoot Horses, Don't They?* (1969) and her Oscar-winning characterization of Bree Daniels in Alan Pakula's *Klute* (1971) did not open the magic gates of Tinseltown; activist Jane Fonda had to fight even to get on American screens.

Faye Dunaway and William Holden in Sydney Lumet's NETWORK (1976).

Some sense of the loss American cinema suffered by excluding Jane Fonda can be garnered from a lengthy and revealing interview with director Alan Pakula published in the Spring 1972 issue of *Sight and Sound,* in which he details Fonda's dedication to analyzing the role of Bree, her intuitive sense of this complex character, and her uncanny ability to draw up emotions from deep within her psyche as she improvises. Many of the quiet moments in *Klute* were Fonda's inspirations; she contributed, for example, the little hymn Bree hums. And Bree's moving breakthrough with her female therapist was, as Pakula recalls it, also a dramatic breakthrough for the actress: "Jane burst into tears and everything came pouring out, ninety per cent of what I have in the film, and she said, 'You know what it is? I'm beginning to *feel*. And I'm just so scared.' It came out, the voice was shaking, it was happening, and my back went up like *that!* . . . There was no way of directing that, everthing pouring out. . . . And then we ran out of film."

For four or five years, Fonda herself was almost out of film, scrounging around for roles in minor projects like the low-budget, high-spirited *Steelyard Blues* (1972), an amusing toast to anarchy; the poorly executed Joseph Losey version of *A Doll's House* (1973), an impassioned though dated plea for women's liberation; the infrequently exhibited *FTA* (1974), a counter-cultural USO show that told soldiers what to do with the Army; and George Cukor's *The Blue Bird* (1976), a multimillion dollar lead balloon that sent other Soviet-American cinematic ventures back to the drawing boards.

Producers Peter Bart and Max Palevsky offered Jane Fonda her first big chance to work in a major production in 1977, when they selected her for their satire, *Fun with Dick and Jane,* a comic post-Vietnam recession primer on coping with chronic unemployment, corporate embezzlement, and wholesale corruption. Dick (George Segal) and Jane (Jane Fonda), the typical American couple, live in a Benedict Canyon tract house; it is a dream house on the outside, but inside, as the producers observed, "everything was cheap and flimsy, programmed to fall apart in ten or fifteen years. . . . It has a phoniness—a tackiness—which we wouldn't dare try to duplicate on a sound stage." When the aerospace industry collapses, Dick and Jane must cope with austerity. Her suggesting that they drop the book club in the face of adversity just does not suffice, so they turn to robbery as

Jane Fonda and George Segal in Ted Kotcheff's FUN WITH DICK AND JANE (1977).

a source of income. Cheered as folk heroes when they assail the telephone company, eventually they fleece the company that fired Dick while it kept two sets of ledgers and paid illegal bribes to foreign officials. Audiences applauded the many gags in *Fun with Dick and Jane*, while Jane could rejoice in its deeper level: "Even at its funniest, it takes a long overdue look at a situation in which many Americans have found themselves."

Light comedy or serious commentary, director Ted Kotcheff's feature launched Fonda on a meteoric climb to eminence in Hollywood. Her six roles in the next three years established her as the reigning queen of Hollywood, the nation's most outstanding acting talent. *Julia* (1977), for example, gave America a new look at the early history of the long-exiled Lillian Hellman, who managed to survive a time of scoundrels to return triumphantly to the Academy Awards ceremony as a living legend. Cast as the young aspiring playwright, Jane Fonda brings a poignancy to a gentle romance with a crotchety Dashiell Hammett, skillfully portrayed by Jason Robards, an actor who improves with each passing year. In *Julia*, Fonda demonstrated her mastery of the critical lesson in acting: "In the beginning you try too hard and end up by showing too much. It's only later that you learn if you are truly experiencing and behaving, then it doesn't show." Fonda hides her art as she nervously carries contraband across a border, smashes cigarettes by her typewriter, or squeezes Julia's hand for luck; she makes audiences see what her character is feeling without letting them notice the magic of her performance.

Fonda won the Oscar she coveted more than any other for *Coming Home* (1978), her powerful antiwar statement set at a veteran's hospital. Everyone in Hollywood knew what she meant when she told the press afterward that "we've gone through a lot"; as she so aptly noted, "there was a time when certain people wanted to put me in jail. Now they've gone to jail and I'm still working." Fonda's work at the end of the decade proved quite substantial and artistically rewarding. In *Comes a Horseman* (1978), she joined director Alan Pakula in a project marred by an inadequate script whose deficiencies are all the more notable since Fonda is so good as Ella Connors. She manages to turn an awkward confession of her seduction and humiliation by J. W. Ewing (Jason Robards) into a moving account of the collapse of youthful illusions and paternal pride; this same passion explodes as

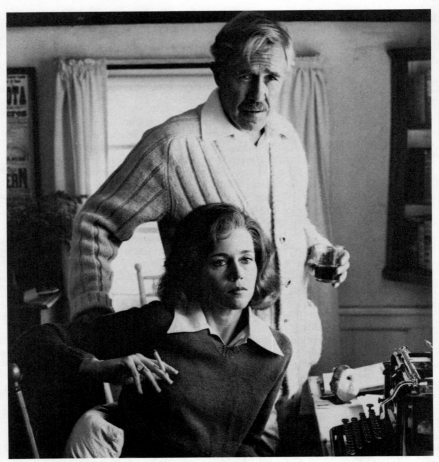

Jane Fonda and Jason Robards in Fred Zinnemann's JULIA (1977).

she and Frank Athearn (James Caan) fix a windmill and again witness J. W.'s cruel power.

For director Herbert Ross, the forty-two-year-old Fonda donned a bikini and checked into Neil Simon's *California Suite* (1978) as the self-assured, independent Hannah Warren, a small but powerful role that compresses a wide range of emotions into a very short time span. Fonda brought an intensity to her encounters with ex-husband Bill (Alan Alda) not evident in the Bill Cosby-Richard Pryor or Walter Matthau-Elaine May segments; only the Michael Caine-Maggie Smith episode seemed on a par with the Fonda-Alda performances.

In *The China Syndrome* (1979), all the cast worked at high energy levels, including an inspired Jack Lemmon and a confident Mike Douglas, the multitalented son of Kirk Douglas who also produced the film. Director Jim Bridges' original notes for the production included the jottings "Electronic woman . . . media man . . . high priest to the monster . . . a monster film," and later accounts suggest that everyone involved knew this "monster" was about to attack in real life. Jane Fonda and the whole production unit recognized that the "no nuke" movement was the new antiwar campaign of the late Seventies and Eighties. Jane Fonda was once again unafraid to lead the troops, even though the boycott began again. General Electric withdrew its sponsorship, for example, of the March 13, 1979, Barbara Walters interview show on ABC because of a segment with Jane Fonda; the company's press statement blithely explained it was "inappropriate" for GE to sponsor a program containing "material that could cause undue public concern about nuclear power."

Even as Jane Fonda starred with Robert Redford in the provocative *The Electric Horseman* (1979), new opposition to her and her husband, politician Tom Hayden, mounted. On the eve of the 1980 election, the California Senate refused to confirm Jane Fonda's appointment to the California Arts Council, without granting the two-time Academy Award winner a chance to testify. In Dalton Trumbo's immortal words, it was once again "the time of the toad." More than three hundred celebrities took out a newspaper ad supporting Jane Fonda, but even the collective voice of Alan Alda, Woody Allen, Jack Nicholson, Burt Reynolds, and Mel Brooks could not convince the yahoos of the State Senate that Jane Fonda was a qualified representative of the arts.

Jane Fonda in Hal Ashby's COMING HOME (1978).

If Jane Fonda was the queen of Hollywood actresses, there were several quite remarkable ladies-in-waiting, whose achievements in the Seventies augured well for the Eighties. Jill Clayburgh, for example, overcame the inanities of *Portnoy's Complaint* (1972), *The Thief Who Came to Dinner* (1973), and *Gable and Lombard* (1976) to do some outstanding comedic turns in *The Silver Streak* (1977) and *Semi-Tough* (1977). She ended the decade with stunning performances in Paul Mazursky's *An Unmarried Woman* (1978), Bernardo Bertolucci's magnificently photographed and somewhat scandalous *La Luna* (1979), a mixture of opera and incest, and Alan Pakula's comic variation on *An Unmarried Woman, Starting Over* (1979), featuring Burt Reynolds as a man divorced by his wife.

Meryl Streep, who played Anne Marie in *Julia* (1977), a small but memorable performance, also made her limited participation in *The Deer Hunter* (1978) seem larger and more important than it was; she converts Linda's clumsy attempts at communication into something truly precious. Woody Allen's *Manhattan* (1979) included another effective walk-on for Streep, but as Karen Traynor in *The Seduction of Joe Tynan* (1979), she transcends Alan Alda's script, charming audiences with a Southern accent as rich as praline candy and a passion as spicy as Creole gumbo. *Kramer vs. Kramer* (1979) limited her main appearances to the beginning, the custody hearing, and end, but Meryl Streep still managed to project a more appealing presence than the original characterization in Avery Corman's best seller. This Yale Drama School graduate told *New York Times* interviewer Janet Maslin that she looks forward to bigger parts in the future, but she rules out "soft core" scripts where her character "emerges in half-light, half dressed." It's not that Meryl Streep is prudish, but she knows those characters do not "even have a name until they [the screenwriters] write the third draft." Meryl Streep wants her women to have names and identities, not just good looks.

Sissy Spacek was not averse to putting her freckled body on display in Michael Ritchie's *Prime Cut* (1972), Brian De Palma's *Carrie* (1976), and Alan Randolph's *Welcome to L.A.* (1977), but she too was very careful to choose substantial roles in widely discussed projects. As Holly, Spacek controlled the narrative in Terrence Malick's *Badlands* (1974). Her characterization of Pinky provided the fulcrum for Millie (Shelley Duvall) and Willie (Janice Rule) in *Three Women*

*Jill Clayburgh in
Arthur Hiller's
SILVER STREAK
(1977).*

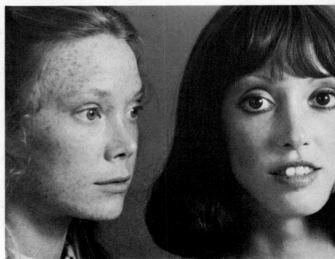

*Sissy Spacek and
Shelley Duvall in
Robert Altman's
THREE WOMEN
(1977).*

Meryl Streep in Michael Cimino's THE DEER HUNTER (1978).

(1977), just as her Carolyn Cassady played a central role in *Heart Beat* (1980).

As *Time* magazine reported in its August 13, 1979, issue, there is a whole new generation of "whiz kids" in Hollywood waiting for just such a lucky break, including such precocious adolescents as Brooke Shields (*Pretty Baby*, 1978; *Just You and Me, Kid*, 1979; *Tilt*, 1979), Tatum O'Neal (*Paper Moon*, 1973; *International Velvet*, 1978), Mariel Hemingway (*Lipstick*, 1976; *Manhattan*, 1979), and Linda Manz (*Days of Heaven*, 1978; *The Wanderers*, 1979). And as these juvenile actresses waited, an octagenarian performer, who once ruled Hollywood, could not resist the glitter of the tinsel, so she made one further foray on to the screen in the poorly received *Sextette* (1978). The old innuendoes and sexual grotesqueries no longer charmed audiences into "coming up and seeing" a female performer. In the Seventies, what women did and said was more important than their looks.

6. Gonna Fly Now

> *And it's all so cruel and capricious – one*
> *minute you're a kind of Culture Hero and the*
> *next minute everybody's forgotten you. And the*
> *people you have to pander to, the Great*
> *American audience . . . a hundred million*
> *goons!*
> IRWIN SHAW, *Evening in Byzantium*

IN AUGUST OF 1979, the legal council for the Wrather Corporation won a ruling from a Los Angeles court which forbade sixty-four-year-old Clayton Moore to wear a mask "identical to or markedly similar to" the Lone Ranger disguise he had worn for ten years in films and on television. Wrather owned the rights to the saga of the Lone Ranger, and wanted to say "Adios, Kemo Sabe" to Moore, whose real aging might confuse audiences familiar with the fantasy of the eternally young and vibrant champion of human rights, his faithful sidekick Tonto, and his sprightly white stallion Silver. Wrather was planning a new movie, and an old masked avenger just would not do, even if he was in superb physical condition.

Hollywood in the Seventies seemed intent on becoming the "used plot lot" Richard Dyer MacCann jested about, resurrecting old genres and trying to fill them with new life. Herbert Marcuse, the Marxist theorist who died at the end of the decade, could not have postulated a more paradigmatic capitalist response to a failing domestic economy, a president who resigned in disgrace, an ill-advised war that ended in defeat, and an energy crisis that just would not go away. In the face of these travails, conglomerate-controlled popular culture brought back all the old fantasies and created a few new horrors to overshadow real ones. Astute social critics like Gore Vidal quickly saw through the charade, but few members of the mass audience accepted his perspicuous assessment of films like *Jaws:* "Such movies distract people from the thoughts of the robbery and deceit to which they are subjected daily by oil companies, politicians, and banks." For most Americans, the genre exercises of the Seventies seemed mindless,

183

enjoyable escapes, not the awful entrapments and eviscerations Marcuse and others decried.

Seventies America wallowed in *The Culture of Narcissism,* content with solipsistic fantasies fed by Hollywood. British critic David Thomson outlined many of the key themes in contemporary American film in his fine study *America in the Dark,* subtitled *Hollywood and the Gift of Unreality* (William Morrow and Company, 1977), where he commented on the essential self-absorption of fantasy, "the loneliest reach of the imagination where we are desert island monarchs, torn between the perfection in which everything yields to our whim and the terrible lack of company," and questioned how much "Hollywood's criteria for narrative—that it be immediately comprehensible, resolved, and tidy," influenced American philosophy, taste, and policies. Journalist-raconteur Aaron Latham provided an excellent case study on these same themes in his important *Esquire* article, "Life in a Co-ed Animal House," a scathing portrait of "the fantasy generation," the spaced-out collegiate sons and daughters of "me decade" parents, siblings so nervous about the decline of American affluence, hard times in the job market, and grim futures that they embraced grotesque costumes and mindless hedonism, food fights and toga parties, Saturday night fever and discoland, where the music never stopped.

No clearer indication of the rejection of social activism and the return of self-absorption exists than the cycle of sports films initiated by Sylvester Stallone's *Rocky* (1976). In an age of body culture, jogging, organic food, Perrier water, and Adidas shoes, "the Italian Stallion" appealed to both the born-again readers of *Prevention* magazine and the transcendental prophets of *Runner* magazine, to jock culture and the Esalen set. *Rocky* made the steps of the Philadelphia Art Museum a more popular tourist attraction than the Liberty Bell.

Rocky Balboa uncovered vast new oceans for Hollywood producers when he fought (*Rocky*), then conquered (*Rocky II*) the symbolically named Apollo Creed (Carl Weathers); rumor has it this defeated Ali surrogate will be in the champ's corner when the Philadelphia brawler risks his crown in a match set in the Roman Coliseum (*Rocky III?*). In addition to these authorized sequels (some critics call them repeats), *Rocky* launched a flood of spinoffs that plagiarized Stallone's quasimythical tale of an inarticulate, stunted, handicapped

Sylvester Stallone and Carl Weathers in John Avildsen's ROCKY (1976).

lover who transforms his frustrations into victory and romance. Rocky and the legions of Rocky icons were Nixon's "tough" Americans who "got going" when "the going got tough."

No sport seemed immune to a Rocky-style rendition—not bowling (*The Dreamer,* 1979), basketball (*One on One,* 1977), or ice skating (*Ice Castles,* 1978); not professional wrestling (*The One and Only,* 1978), horse racing (*Casey's Shadow,* 1978), or the Olympics (*Goldengirl,* 1979); not boxing (*The Champ,* 1979; *The Main Event,* 1979), tennis (*Players,* 1979), or the marathon (*Running,* 1979). Even collegiate bicycle racing nurtured an effective *Rocky* variant in *Breaking Away* (1979), Peter Yates's sensitive comedy about the clash between town and gown, "cutters" and collegians. Yates wisely develops the tensions between an all-American family in the heartlands of Indiana and an adventuresome son (Dennis Christopher), enamored first of Italian cyclists, then of French beauties. His father (Paul Dooley) does not want all these "-ini" foods like zucchini, linguine, and fettuccine in his house, cannot stand the operatic hugging and kissing, and seems equally nonplussed by "Ciao" and "Bonjour." For all its stylish comedy, however, *Breaking Away* builds to the big race and the hapless cutter team's battle with impudent, upper-class fraternity brothers, a duel that keeps audiences screaming as the finish line draws near for a battered battler.

Populist savant George Leonard argued in his widely reprinted essay, "The Ultimate Athlete," that these clearly defined struggles are essential for an age of chaos: ". . . the structure provided by sports is especially critical in a time when every other structure seems uncertain . . . we need a mythic sports figure to be our model and guide on the journey that now speeds us toward inconceivable destinations." The aptly named Rocky Balboa and his progeny were such guides for legions of fans in the Seventies; world-class athletes were the scaled-down superheroes for America's shell-shocked grownups.

Young adults and adolescents in the Seventies gravitated towards popular singers and rock superstars as their gurus; music was a convenient shibboleth separating the hearing-aid set from a generation weaned on heavy metal, super amplification, and punk rock. The record business was considerably larger than the movie industry, so conglomerates that plied their wares in both markets rejoiced to see features like *Saturday Night Fever* (1977), *Grease* (1978), and *American Graffiti* (1973) climb both *Billboard*'s sales charts and *Variety*'s

John Travolta in Randal Kleiser's GREASE (1978).

rental listings. The movie advertised the disk, just as the platter sent fans back for a visual performance in the theater.

No wonder Beverly Hills threatened for quite a while to become Tin Pan Alley, Woodstock, Filmore, Carnegie Hall, the Palladium, 2001 Odyssey, and CBGB all rolled into one. Bette Midler left the Continental Baths and the Copacabana behind to play a Janis Joplin type in *The Rose* (1979), while Bob Dylan filmed his Rolling Thunder Revue for his four-hour poetic hegira, *Renaldo and Clara* (1978). Kris Kristofferson might sing of "Easter Island" with Rita Coolidge, but he spent most of his time on soundstages. Even the dark prince of the world's greatest rock and roll band, Mick Jagger, tried his luck in Nicolas Roeg's sinister *Performance* (1970) and Tony Richardson's idiosyncratic *Ned Kelly* (1970). While his estranged wife Bianca sought an appropriately erotic cinematic vehicle in *The American Success Company* (1979), Mick joined Richard Gere and Amy Irving in Michelangelo Antonioni's *Suffer or Die*.

Concert films were all the rage in the Seventies, as the overcrowding at Bethel proved there were more Aquarians looking for three days of peace, love, and harmony than there were communities willing to welcome them. Michael Wadleigh's *Woodstock* (1970) brought Joan Baez, Country Joe and the Fish, and Jimi Hendrix to the millions who missed the mud, fellowship, and good vibes of what *Time* magazine described as "History's Biggest Happening" and "one of the most significant political and sociological events of the age." Warner Brothers gambled one hundred thousand dollars filming the festival with twelve 16-mm cameras that shot 120 hours of film; it took ten times that amount of money to complete the elaborate task of editing and blowing the film up to standard 35-mm. There were hopes that Orion Pictures would commemorate the tenth anniversary of Woodstock with *Woodstock II*, but America had turned inward and community objections to traffic jams, overcrowding, and inconvenience nixed the project; only a few stragglers made the pilgrimage to Max Yasgur's farm on August 15, 1979.

Some of the changes in the American consciousness might be explained by film critic Diane Jacobs' observation that "the history of America in the early Seventies reads something like a lobotomy of the late Sixties," but a good deal hinged on the older generation's fixation with the murder at Altamount so powerfully documented in the

Peace, Love, and Harmony in Michael Wadleigh's WOODSTOCK (1970).

Maysles Brothers' *Gimme Shelter* (1970), and their chronic inability to accept new models of the American psyche, like the Kabuki-masked Kiss (*Attack of the Phantoms*, 1979), the irreverent Mothers of Invention (*200 Motels*, 1971), the epicene David Bowie (*The Man Who Fell to Earth*, 1976), the raucous Ramones (*Rock and Roll High School*, 1979), and the anarchic British rockers, The Who (*The Kids Are Alright*, 1979; *Quadrophenia*, 1979). Oldsters waxed nostalgic about clean-cut American heroes like Elvis Presley, ignoring the notoriety he once generated and the circumstances surrounding his demise, and longed elegiacally for the relative innocent frenzy of Beatlemania (*I Wanna Hold Your Hand*, 1978) in the face of Sid Vicious and his cohorts. Things were clearly escalating when the Band decided to stop touring (*The Last Waltz*, 1978), Bob Dylan sang of Christianity, and troubadour Neil Young prepared a retrospective of his greatest hits (*Rust Never Sleeps*, 1979).

Films of Broadway musicals changed substantially in the Seventies: for every doughty *Mame* (1974) there was a dynamic *Jesus Christ Superstar* (1973). Traditional extravaganzas aimed at Wednesday matinee matrons from the suburbs like *Fiddler on the Roof* (1971) and *The Man of La Mancha* (1972) were giving way to the pop evangelism of *Godspell* (1973), the black rhythms of *The Wiz* (1978), the teen-age daydreams of *Grease* (1978), the discordant chords of the Who's rock opera *Tommy* (1977), and the kinky charms of Bruce Kimmen's forthrightly named *First Nudie Musical* (1976).

Two cinematic musicals dominate the decade, however: *Cabaret* (1972), which won Bob Fosse the best director Oscar and Geoffrey Unsworth the best cinematographer Oscar, and *Hair* (1979), America's tribal musical as interpreted by Milos Forman. *Cabaret*, as Pauline Kael astutely noted, turned the conventions of big musical movies "inside out": "the floor show at the Kit Kat Klub is used as a prism through which we see the characters' lives." Joel Gray, Liza Minnelli, and Michael York translate Christopher Isherwood's literary themes to the screen just as melodiously as they handle the music by John Kander and the lyrics by Fred Ebb. In *Hair*, Forman overcomes the problem of dated materials by relying on inventive camerawork that makes horses dance almost as well as the humans moving to Twyla Tharp's choreography and by creating considerable artistic distance between his production and the original show; the innovative

Liza Minnelli and Joel Grey in Bob Fosse's CABARET (1972).

191

Czech director attributed the good spirits in his cinematic adaptation to a conscious historical detachment: "Distance gave us the freedom to see the era in perspective and made us able to laugh at things considered sacred."

Historical distance also made possible some outstanding biographies of musicians and other artists, including Sidney J. Furie's laundered account of the life of black superstar Billie Holiday, *Lady Sings the Blues* (1972), the one role that demonstrated the huge talents of Diana Ross; photographer-turned-filmmaker Gordon Parks's incendiary homage to Huddie Ledbetter, *Leadbelly* (1976), which follows America's great folk songwriter from Fannin Street in Shreveport to fame and then imprisonment in Angola Prison; and Floyd Mutrux' daring chronicle of the rise of rock and roll and the persecution of Alan Freed, *American Hot Wax* (1978). Gary Busey offered one of the finest performances of the decade as a gangly, spectacled Texas boy with a buck-toothed smile, tons of charm, and a whole new approach to harmony in *The Buddy Holly Story* (1978), a B movie leavened by grade-A talent, while David Carradine had the thankless task of portraying Woody Guthrie in Hal Ashby's *Bound for Glory* (1976), where Haskell Wexler's camera is the real star.

George de la Pena assayed the title role in Herbert Ross's *Nijinsky* (1980), a daring attempt to explore Vaslav Nijinsky's art, his tortured relationship with Sergei Diaghilev, and his marriage; Ross hoped, he asserted, "to try and explain the mystery of his madness and his agony over his bisexuality in a sensitive and sympathetic way." Director Bob Fosse obviously was just as sympathetic to his hero in the autobiographical *All That Jazz* (1979), which features a grand performance by Roy Scheider impersonating choreographer Fosse and interesting portrayals by Gwen Verdon and Ann Lange in characterizations molded on their own lives. Unfortunately, Fosse's total conception alienated audiences with its nihilism and egoism.

Some Hollywood stars were even less blessed in their biographies; William Claude Dukinfield is still probably spinning in his grave, glad to be anywhere rather than in *W. C. Fields and Me* (1976), Rod Steiger's classic demonstration that good acting must be more than an extended impersonation. Based on the memoirs of Carlotta Monti, played by Valerie Perrine, *W. C. Fields and Me* is just the sort of memorial Fields might have wished for Baby LeRoy. Clark Gable and

Carole Lombard fare no better as reincarnated by James Brolin and Jill Clayburgh in *Gable and Lombard* (1976), Sidney J. Furie's uneven combination of smut and sentimentality. James Dean is the abiding presence in *9/30/55* (1977), a flawed but intriguing exploration of celebrity and its influence on a decade, written and directed by James Bridges, and sabotaged by a weak performance by Richard Thomas. Hollywood performers were actually best served by the compilation films that celebrated studio anniversaries and the nation's bicentennial; well-chosen clips in *America at the Movies* (1976) and *That's Entertainment, Part One* (1974) and *Part Two* (1976) reminded audiences of the wonders of American cinema.

Black performers like Sidney Poitier, James Earl Jones, and Bill Cosby, black writers like Ralph Ellison, John Killens, and James Baldwin, and black directors like Gordon Parks, Melvin Van Peebles, and Michael Schultz were assailing that same Hollywood tradition for creating a distorted image of black people. Bill Cosby starred in an effective short showing how black history had been "lost, strayed, or stolen" in films, while critic Donald Bogle gave his interpretive history of blacks in American film the emotionally charged title *Toms, Coons, Mulattoes, Mammies, and Bucks,* an apt summation of his book's central thesis. If the Sixties carried the black struggle to the streets, the Seventies brought it to the screen; black films became an important genre in an age when black patrons were becoming an increasingly large part of the entertainment audience. At first, a spate of "blaxploitation" films tried to ensnare a carefully defined audience, content with mayhem, loud music, tough talk, and fast women; then came more sophisticated "crossover" films, aimed at more discriminating audiences. The television saga of Kunta Kinte in *Roots* had generated the highest Nielsen ratings on American television in the history of the medium; ever-alert and imitative film producers logically sought more gold in the black hills of Africa, the farmlands of the South, and the dark streets of urban ghettos.

In the blighted tradition of blaxploitation, a few titles do stand out. Melvin Van Peebles' *Sweet Sweetback's Baadasss Song* (1971), starring "the black community," may be the most antiwhite establishment film ever rated by the MPAA. The X it received was, Van Peebles charged, one more example of the racism of the system the film attacked. Van Peebles' film warned that its cop-killing hero (Van

Melvin Van Peebles in his SWEET SWEETBACK'S BAADASSSS SONG (1971).

Peebles himself), "a baadasss nigger," was "coming back to collect some dues." Gordon Parks, Jr., directed *Super Fly* one year later, which might well evidence the collection prophesied. Priest (Ron O'Neal) is the hustler-pimp-superstud-pusher as demigod. Resplendently outfitted in soft velvets, stylish suedes, the boldly patterned broadcloths, sporting a tiny pistol and ostentatious jewelry, Priest double-crosses everyone, outwitting the drug establishment and the police to make his big score. He is the new black gangster as hero, with no sense of tragedy at all.

More traditional black variants on gangster motifs include the Shaft series with Richard Roundtree (*Shaft*, 1971; *Shaft's Big Score*, 1972; *Shaft in Africa*, 1973) that emphasize physical daring, well-realized décors, and driving music; two films based on the novels of Chester Himes, *Cotton Comes to Harlem* (1970) and *Come Back Charleston Blue* (1972), both starring Godfrey Cambridge as the droll Gravedigger Jones and Raymond St. Jacques as Coffin Ed Johnson; and Sidney Poitier's further adventures as a San Francisco detective, *They Call Me Mister Tibbs* (1970) and *The Organization* (1971), neither of which lives up to the promise of *In the Heat of the Night* (1969).

As black films prospered, every classic Hollywood formula lent itself to a switch in races. *Blacula* (1972) suggested a new bloodline for the Transylvanian count, while *Blackenstein* (1974) added new dimensions to Mary Shelley's monster. For sports fans, Michael Schultz's *Greased Lightning* (1977) detailed the achievements of Wendell Scott (Richard Pryor) in automobile racing, while John Badham's *The Bingo Long Traveling All Stars and Motor Kings* (1976) loaded the bases with William Brashler's hysterical tale of a renegade group of black baseball stars who scoured the Midwest looking for games with white teams and the best of the Negro National League. Sidney Poitier made the best black Western of the decade, *Buck and the Preacher* (1972), which skillfully suggested the affinities between emancipated slaves fleeing the South and nomadic Indians seeking security in the West: here was a Western where the villains were marauding white men terrorizing men of color.

Poitier also made the most successful "crossover" films of the Seventies, a series of stylish comedies that mirrored the new affluence of some blacks. His heroes in *Uptown Saturday Night* (1974) and *Let's Do It Again* (1975) were working-class buddies who knew how

195

*Sheila Frazier and
Ryan O'Neal in
Gordon Parks, Jr.'s
SUPER FLY (1972).*

*Sidney Poitier and
Harry Belafonte in
Poitier's BUCK
AND THE
PREACHER
(1972).*

to live it up when the lottery picked their number or when there was a confidence game to be executed. They dine ostentatiously in the most opulent of surroundings, sport eye-catching clothes from the boldest of haberdashers, and relish the manifold delights of Madame Xenobia's pleasure palace. Even in Poitier's overly preachy *A Piece of the Action* (1977), his shady heroes (Bill Cosby and Sidney Poitier) impress a group of young thugs more with their money, clothes, cars, and women than with their modesty and philanthropy. Poitier was quite attuned to the materialistic cravings of black and white Americans; he loads his films with silk suits, designer dresses, and conspicuous consumption. Audiences flocked to these wish-fulfillment fantasies, colorful, extravagant variations on the American dream.

Outside observers have often charged that the love of possessions is a sickness with the American people, and Hollywood developed a new genre in the Seventies to capitalize on audience fixations with material things: the decade's mammoth disaster epics were the flip side of the American dream, chilling, nightmarish visions of transience. The most famous purveyor of disaster, the fabulously wealthy Irwin Allen, told interviewers that nightmare was his "best source of entertainment"; his epic productions resulted from intense personal visions of catastrophe: "During the night I do have these nightmares and live these fantasies. And by the side of my bed, I have a big pad and several pencils, and when I wake I make notes that finally result in film material." Allen gave American consumers a world turned upside down when a tidal wave disrupted the voyage of a luxurious ocean liner in *The Poseidon Adventure* (1972), a world in flames in *The Towering Inferno* (1974), an all-star melodrama about an expensive skyscraper engulfed by fire, and a world under attack, as the "killer bees" overran missile silos and the Sun Belt in *The Swarm* (1978). No natural catastrophe escaped the purview of Hollywood's craftsmen. Charlton Heston's heroics barely ameliorated the terror of *Earthquake* (1974); there was no answer to the insects in *The Hellstrom Chronicle* (1971); and little remained of Manhattan after *Meteor* (1979). Alvin Rakoff's *City on Fire* (1979) combined "the force of an earthquake" and "the flames of a thousand infernos" in a film advertised as "the disaster epic that towers above them all." If film makers were to be trusted, America was heading down *Damnation Alley* (1977), and everyone was facing a *Cassandra Crossing* (1978). Even sports fans were not safe; this could always be *Black*

Sunday (1977), and there might not be any *Two Minute Warning* (1976); terrorists were riding the *Rollercoaster* (1977), and who knew when *The Boys From Brazil* (1978) might grow up?

Paralleling this onslaught of cataclysmic doom was a stunning renaissance of horror films. New film audiences were hooked on the vicarious thrills of massive destruction and graphic visions of the unspeakably horrendous. Young film goers seemed hypnotized by the theme song of the British-made *The Rocky Horror Picture Show* (1975), a film most popular at midnight screenings: "Toucha, toucha, toucha, touch me/I wanna be dirty; Thrill me, fill me, fulfill me/ Creature of the night." Orion Pictures' cerebral executive vice-president Mike Medavoy offered a traditional psychoanalytic explanation for this thirst for terror: "People are fixated with horror. We're digging deep in the Freudian psyche. It's an escape from reality; for some people, maybe reality is boring." Even disconcerting fantasies seemed more enticing than the energyless America of Jimmy Carter.

Several fine young directors, including Brian De Palma, George Romero, and John Carpenter, devoted their best skills to creating shudders. De Palma's masterpiece is *Sisters* (1973), a Hitchcockian tale of Siamese twins, insanity, and savage murder, errily photographed by Gregory Sandor with an effective score by Bernard Herrmann. The film proved too dense with allusions and was rife with too much black comedy for audiences who liked more straightforward shocks. De Palma's *Phantom of the Paradise* (1975) also failed to find its audience; horror buffs were not attuned to his Faustian visions of the record business. *Carrie* (1976) hit just the right combination of sexual anxiety, teen-age insecurity, and vengeful poltergeist to assure De Palma's future in films; *The Fury* (1978) was more of the same, with some Oedipal elements thrown in, better special effects, and an explosive conclusion. After all this gore, De Palma took a short vacation teaching film at Sarah Lawrence, where he supervised the independent feature, *Home Movies* (1980).

George Romero, the king of the independents, never seemed to tire of blood and guts. The *auteur* who came to prominence with the cannibalistic atomic zombies of *The Night of the Living Dead* (1968) continued to churn out violent attacks on pollution and government ineptitude, *The Crazies* (1973), and bloody visions of contemporary vampires, *Martin* (1975); Romero's *pièce de résistance*, however, was his sequel, *Dawn of the Dead* (1978), which turned his zombies loose on the cradle of American consumption, the shopping mall. Romero refused to submit *Dawn of the Dead* for an MPAA rating, complaining bitterly that an X would imply a sexuality the film lacks; his self-imposed X was merely an acknowledgment that its bloodier scenes might drive even a professional reviewer to the exit.

Romero loves to talk about his films. *Dawn of the Dead,* he argues, has its philosophical side; in his view, the zombies represent "us": "all the monsters we've created in fiction . . . represent our own evil. We create them so we can kill them off, thereby justifying ourselves—it's a kind of penance, a self-exorcism." Romero works with his own partners, the Laurel Group, largely because he wants to avoid the snares of big productions: "I don't want to make movies so I can live in Hollywood. I don't want to make deals so that I can make movies. I want to make movies. Period."

John Carpenter, another patron saint of the *cinéma fantastique,* is just as addicted to celluloid as Romero, but Carpenter longs for the bygone days of Hollywood backlots: "If I had three wishes, one of them would be, 'Send me back to the Forties and the studio system and let me direct movies.' Because I would have been happiest there." Carpenter's *Halloween* (1978) is no studio production, but it is a stunning example of how much horror can be found in dark houses when a murderous psychopath is out to slaughter smooching teenagers and innocent babysitters. Carpenter's *The Fog* (1979) is a riveting ghost story set on the California coast, about drowned sailors who come back to get their revenge, which features Carpenter's wife, Adrienne Barbeau, as a disc jockey in an isolated lighthouse confronting "a terror no human being should ever have to see again."

Author William Goldman tried his hand at psychological horror for Joseph Levine in Richard Attenborough's *Magic* (1978), a thriller about an introverted ventriloquist and his foul-mouthed dummy. Just when Corky (Anthony Hopkins) is about to make the big time, he panics and retreats to his old home, where he tries to recapture the storybook romance that eluded him in high school. His old flame, Peggy Ann Snow (Ann-Margret), and his new master, dummy Fats, soon vie for Corky's love and their own lives.

Magic is, of course, a variation on Alberto Cavalcanti's "Ventriloquist," the most effective episode in the 1945 British thriller,

Ann-Margret and Anthony Hopkins in Richard Attenborough's MAGIC (1978).

Dead of Night. The Seventies witnessed a great number of remakes and reinterpretations of classic horror stories. Andy Warhol produced two of the bloodiest films ever in his three-dimension/Technicolor *Frankenstein* (1974), starring Joe Dallesandro as the well-endowed field hand and Monique Van Vooren as the voluptuous baroness, and his X-rated *Dracula* (1974), in which the sexually active field hand Dallesandro confronts a cadaverous villain (Udo Kier). Frank Langella played a more full-bodied and charismatic predator in John Badham's adaptation of the Broadway smash, *Dracula* (1979). Badham develops the Freudian aspects of Bram Stoker's classic tale; Langella's shape shifter seems just as at home in the boudoir as the crypt, and his best bloodsucking comes only after some rather heavy necking.

Not all the horror in the Seventies emerged from the shadowy past; science fiction provided its own transfusion of cheap thrills and cosmic blues. *Alien,* the summer box-office champ in 1979, transported audiences to the seventh decade of the Twenty-first Century to meet the ultimate killing machine, as envisioned by the Swiss artist of the bizarre, H. R. Giger. *Alien* was not, its co-author Dan O'Bannon admitted, a "think piece"; the message he intended was simple: "Don't close your eyes or it will get ya." Seventies heroes also had to keep their eyes open in Philip Kaufman's remake of *The Invasion of the Body Snatchers* (1978) or the pods would have them. Kaufman weaves some interesting commentary about trendy pop psychology around Jack Finney's paranoid fantasy, but his emphasis on the mechanics of transformation make the unearthly threat as physical as it is mental. Even when a dog and an old man are fused in one pod by error, there is none of the playfulness of *Star Wars* (1977) or *Close Encounters* (1977). As producer Robert Solo observed, *Invasion of the Body Snatchers* is not "any Star Spores"; its conclusion is not medals for heroes, but agonizing betrayal and all-devouring darkness.

The same somber tone and ultimate abandonment is evidenced in L. Q. Jones's adaptation of Harlan Ellison's novella, *A Boy and His Dog* (1976), a curious amalgam of realistic suffering and a surrealistic plot. *A Boy and His Dog* labors much too obviously to make its clumsy condemnations of small-town American values. A similarly inept tendentiousness mars Michael Anderson's *Logan's Run* (1976), which demonstrated that superb special effects and gorgeous women (Jerry Agutter and Farrah Fawcett) cannot conceal an aged plot;

Tom Skerritt, Harry Dean Stanton and Veronica Cartwright
in ALIEN

Richard Fleischer's *Soylent Green* (1973), which enmeshed Charlton Heston for ninety minutes in a mystery audiences solved in five; and Bryan Forbes's *The Stepford Wives* (1975), which showed it was hard to tell Katharine Ross playing a robot from Katharine Ross playing a normal housewife.

The Russian foreign correspondent for *Izvestia*, Melor Sturva, was disturbed by the "anti-Soviet symbolism dressed in a transparent tunic of science fiction" he discovered in two theatrical features culled from television screens, *Battlestar Galactica* (1979) and *Buck Rogers in the Twenty-fifth Century* (1979), but American audiences clearly showed more partiality to the less thematic, more tangible excitement of Walt Disney Productions' spectacular *Black Hole* (1979) and Paramount's long-awaited *Star Trek: the Motion Picture* (1979), the two big Christmas films at the end of the decade. Disney's account of the voyage of the Palomino, a NASA explorer craft, depends heavily on its multimillion dollar special effects, mounted by Peter Ellenshaw, who previously designed both *Mary Poppins* (1964) and *Twenty Thousand Leagues Under the Sea* (1954). Ellenshaw was responsible for the striking conception of the starship *Cygnus*, which the Palomino discovers drifting toward a collapsed sun. *Star Trek: the Motion Picture* brings all the old crew back to the *Enterprise* for a special mission. Unlike its television predecessors, this holiday fare had a generous budget, and the producers clearly hoped to create a whole new generation of Trekkies. Star William Shatner argued that *Star Trek: the Motion Picture* really existed in a different dimension than all its competitors: "We at *Star Trek* are human beings who try to deal with philosophical questions. Mankind [is pictured] in a space adventure." Fortunately, there was just as much adventure as there was humanism in *Star Trek: the Motion Picture*.

Action and insight were also well balanced in Seventies permutations of the war film genre. Big guns and battlefield heroics dominated traditional sagas like Joseph Sargent's *MacArthur* (1977), Gregory Peck's failed attempt to imitate George C. Scott's *Patton* (1970); Jack Smight's *Midway* (1976), the only sensible use of Sensurround, a sound system that set theaters quaking to bass vibrations as loud as cannon fire; Richard Fleischer's *Tora! Tora! Tora!* (1970), an elephantine recreation of the attack on Pearl Harbor that merited the Oscar for best special visual effects; and Samuel Fuller's *The Big Red One*, a moving study of the "four horsemen" of one squad in the First Infantry Division as they make their way from North Africa into Germany and Czechoslovakia. There were also big movies about the human side of warfare, including John Schlesinger's *Yanks* (1979), a nostalgic look at the third front massing for the Normandy invasion in the desolate villages of England and the romance between local women and foreign infantrymen; Michael Cimino's *The Deer Hunter* (1978), an award-winning study of some steel-mill workers who leave Clairton, Pennsylvania, for the psychic roulette of war in Indochina; and Sidney Furie's *The Boys in Company C* (1978), a scabrous portrait of marines coming of age in a combat zone.

Many of the most shocking "war movies" in the Seventies detailed the aftermath of combat for the American soldier. Vietnam was not the Second World War and, in the movies, these were not "the best years of our lives." *Tracks* (1977), for example, directed and written by Henry Jaglom, followed the odyssey of a sergeant (Dennis Hopper) who had a casket full of horror to share with his countrymen. *Rolling Thunder* (1977), written by Paul Schrader, pictured a Major Charles Rane (William Devane) who had learned all too well how to avenge wrongs. Black vets like Green Beret captain Gordon Hudson returned to America to discover their families ravaged by drugs, so they had no choice but to launch their own crusade in *Gordon's War* (1972), directed by Ossie Davis. Even superpatriot Elia Kazan presented *The Visitors* (1972) back from Vietnam as rapists and despoilers. When Johnny came marching home in the Seventies, he often confirmed the pacifist precept, "the only winner in a war against facism is a fascist."

Some traditional Hollywood genres did not thrive in the Seventies, largely because television preempted most of their materials. The rapacious appetite of the three networks for clear, easily understandable formulas, flexible enough for multitudinous variations, but rigid enough to satisfy audience preconceptions, made the easily assimilated conventions of the Western, the detective story, and the soap opera the principal vehicles for their seven-days-a-week commercial bombardment. To sell soap, a motley assortment of gunslingers, gunsels, and goo inundated America's living rooms; Dodge City, the underworld, and Peyton Place soon became the regular, mundane haunts of armchair-bound snackers. In the face of this almost interminable onslaught of posses, prowlers, and perverts, Hollywood was hard put to find distinctive projects that had not already been gobbled up by television syndicators.

Western films were especially hard hit by the twenty-three and forty-six minute long competitors; *Bonanza, Gunsmoke,* and myriad others had tilled the Western plains rather thoroughly. As *Variety* noted in its June 9, 1979, review of the juvenile *The Apple Dumpling Gang Rides Again* (a title that suggests how dumpy Westerns had become), the only studio "turning out Westerns with any frequency" was Walt Disney Productions, who were aiming at "the moppet sagebrush crowd." The oldest and most revered publishers of Western novels were offering prizes of twenty thousand dollars for the most original concept in a new Western adventure by decade's end.

Most of the popular Westerns in the Seventies were offbeat projects like Ralph Nelson's *Soldier Blue* (1970), an exposé of United States cavalry atrocities; Jan Troell's *Zandy's Bride* (1974), a gloomy look at hard times during the Western migration; and Elliot Silverstein's sensationalized glimpse of Indian ritual, *A Man Called Horse* (1970), which generated the equally savage sequel, *The Return of a Man Called Horse* (1971). The Western myth and ethos was gradually being transformed into a conscious style, a trendy fashion, as the Marlboro Man climbed down off his tall horse to open his "country store," a mail-order boutique inviting country and western fans to emulate their commercial heroes. The Lone Star Cafe emerged as Manhattan's downtown, down-home answer to the uptown, upscale world of Studio 54.

Television series like *Kojak, Charlie's Angels, Columbo,* and *Baretta* also cut deeply into the number of detective films being made. Stars like Eastwood or Bronson might carry a project but, more and more, routine murder and mayhem was becoming the province of the purveyors of Kraft cheese and Charmin toilet tissue. Mysteries with a good gimmick, however, did make it to the screen. Robert Aldrich's *The Choirboys* (1977), for example, had enough kinky sex and raunchy revelations for theatrical release. Milton Katselas' *Report to the Commissioner* (1975) found the proper level of titillation and tension by pitting an innocent white cop (Michael Moriarty) against a streetwise black (Tony King) with an undercover agent (Susan Blakely) as the bait. Peter Yates's *The Friends of Eddie Coyle* (1973)

Peter Boyle and Robert Mitchum in Peter Yates' THE FRIENDS OF EDDIE COYLE (1973).

depended on finely nuanced performances by actors Robert Mitchum and Peter Boyle, the moody photography of Victor J. Kemper, and the low-key surprises of a fine novel by George Higgins. Ted Kotcheff's *Who Is Killing the Great Chefs of Europe?* (1978) offered the diverse charms of the captivating Jacqueline Bisset and the pompously civilized Robert Morley, as well as an epicurean Grand Tour of Europe; the circuit of Joseph Sargent's *The Taking of Pelham One Two Three* (1974) was limited to the Lexington Avenue line, but this subterranean thriller really moved full throttle on an express track.

Among the less popular detective capers in the Seventies, three major ventures deserved greater exposure. Sydney Pollack's *The Yakuza* (1975), based on a screenplay by Paul Schrader and Robert Towne, was shot with both an American and a Japanese crew, and, as the director noted, the sequences in Japan have a quite distinctive look because of differences in lighting techniques: "They don't have large lighting units like we have, so they light the way they paint, an area at a time." Notable contrasts in Japanese and American approaches to the honorable relationships among gang members and to the martial arts are highlighted in this narrative about an aging American gangster (Robert Mitchum) and his Japanese counterpart (Takakura Ken). Director Pollack is especially successful in his careful intercutting of their contrasting fighting styles: "Mitchum is an absolute bull and Ken is like a matador. . . . Mitchum literally walks through paper walls, crashing through them swinging his guns, whereas in another room Ken is poised, kind of catlike, dealing with a whole group." By the end of *The Yakuza*, each man has given painful testimony of his respect for the other.

Arthur Penn's *Night Moves* (1975) demands respect for its aspirations and complexities. Like the "knight move" a championship chess player missed in the heat of combat, but discovered later in an analysis of the match, and then lamented all his life, this existential drama seems more intriguing and rewarding long after it is viewed than it does when it is first being screened. Arthur Penn consciously sought this effect; his convoluted story of the entrapment of investigator Harry Moseby (Gene Hackman) in a plot he understands tragically late is his Watergate puzzle, a mystery in which audiences are not supposed to figure out what happened. As Penn explained in a revealing *Sight and Sound* interview (Spring 1975): "There's a certain

Faye Dunaway and Jack Nicholson in Roman Polanski's CHINATOWN (1975).

eccentricity in almost every interesting case, I think. It doesn't have an explanation, because it's built up of the psychologies of the participants rather than on the circumstantial evidence."

Stuart Rosenberg's *The Drowning Pool* (1975), the second Lew Harper adventure for Paul Newman, also quickly moves beyond the search for a murderer into a bleak exploration of feminine psychology as represented by Iris Devereaux (Joanne Woodward), a Southern oil heiress, Mavis Kilbourne (Gail Strickland), and the oversexed Gretchen (Linda Haynes). The film's climactic scene in a water chamber in an abandoned asylum combines stylish eroticism and a chilling sense of the all-engulfing water, an oceanic tide of corruption and abuse mounting to overwhelm Lew and Mavis, much as J. J. Gittes (Jack Nicholson) and Evelyn Mulwray (Faye Dunaway) are swallowed up in Roman Polanski's *Chinatown* (1975), which was scripted by Robert Towne.

Lovers swimming against an adverse tide are, of course, a staple of soap operas, those curiously elongated melodramas that dominate daytime television, immersing retired pensioners, bored housewives, and truant teenagers in the tortured chronicle of families given to rare tropical diseases, frequent adulteries, and unspeakable social dilemmas. The publishing world's answer to the soaps has long been the gothic novel. Seventies Hollywood merged the two traditions in its own genre, the epic romance, its major attempt to bring cinematic thrills to an audience usually captivated by the small screen, women aged eighteen to thirty-four. Among the notable Seventies romances, Charles Jarrott's *The Other Side of Midnight* (1977) is undoubtedly the most salacious; its heroine, Noelle Page (Marie-France Pisier), sheds lovers and clothes with alarming regularity. Gilbert Cates's *The Promise* (1978) is the most unbelievable; arch-villain Marion (Beatrice Straight) behaves bizarrely enough to outdo the Wicked Witch of the West, and the two lovers (Kathleen Quinlan, Stephen Collins) are separated by, of all things, plastic surgery and an outlandish oath. James Fargo's *Caravans* (1978), based on James Michener's novel, is the most rambling and sententious; the loquacious Zulfigar (Anthony Quinn) constantly spouts the collective wisdom of a nomadic Zorba the Greek, while Mark Miller (Michael Sarrazin) expostulates on the charms of the American way to Ellen Jasper (Jennifer O'Neill), a beautiful maiden torn between two cultures. Women were obviously supposed to swoon at the idea that an older and younger man, Freudian father and son figures, would vie for the oasis of their charms on the scorching sands of the desert.

Hollywood's prime audience, a mix of ages twelve to twenty-four heavily weighted to the bottom of the scale, was not buying any of this mush, even though *Caravans* was set in an exotic locale and larded with gratuitous torture scenes; so the wizards of market research hit upon still another genre patented to provide "ultra-violence" and some of the old "in and out," the teen-age gang-juvenile delinquent fantasy. All the steadfast fans of *Happy Days* were lured to the darker nights of East Coast ghettoes and the lavishly bedecked brotherhoods in Walter Hill's *The Warriors* (1979), Philip Kaufman's *The Wanderers* (1979), and Timothy Galfos' *Sunnyside* (1979); on the West Coast, there was the *barrio machismo* of Robert Collins' *Walk Proud* (1979) and Michael Pressman's *Boulevard Nights* (1979). All these features centered on the need to belong, the will to fight for turf, and the necessity to unite for survival. Their vocabulary was the language of slow-motion violence, with straight-razor-toting lesbians, baseball-bat-wielding Dicky boys, and bald Fordham Bombers lurking everywhere; barely a sequence went by without some adolescent fantasy of mutilation being acted out. Rocks were tied to penises and then dropped great heights, cars were battered and destroyed, and church services turned into rallying points for zealous slashers.

The only drawback haunting these pimple-faced moneymakers was the tendency for overly excited audiences to mimic the goons on screen. The opening run of *The Warriors*, for example, was canceled in Oxnard, California, after a young boy was stabbed to death in the lobby by teenagers. Several other murders followed across the country, theaters were wrecked, and riots ensued during some of the most intense moments. The great American audience was just too carried away by its new culture heroes.

7. It Never Rains in Southern California

*Let's face it, the urge to create a film is
irrational and derives from pure arrogance. . . .
On the screen now it's monsters, or space, or
monsters in space. I'm not sure I care. I don't
believe in a lot anymore. I once did. You had to.
But now—you want to tell it like it is, but when
you find out where it is, they move it.*
STANLEY KRAMER

WHEN EAST COAST novelist Richard Price moved to
Hollywood for a stint as a screenwriter in the traditional odyssey to
"a time in the sun," the one thing he noticed was the health mania of
the natives: "It's so *glamorous,* and everybody's dressed to kill,
everybody's beautiful, and they're all into health food and jogging.
You know why? Because they feel like they might *die any second!*"
Thanatophobia was so endemic to the Seventies that college courses
on dying were quickly oversubscribed, *The Tibetan Book of the Dead*
became a best seller, and Elisabeth Kubler-Ross emerged as the
Florence Nightingale of the age. Even diehard skeptics embraced
a compendium of "true clinical death accounts" entitled *Life
After Death.*

The fixation with death was, after all, just the dark side of the
healthy body cult. Robert Rodale spoke of longevity to Dick Cavett
just before he collapsed and died on television, and Adele Davis, the
guru of feeling well through natural foods, ironically succumbed to the
archenemy of her regimen, cancer. Hero John Wayne and politician
Hubert Humphrey both saw their final agonies make banner headlines
in a perverse nationwide deathwatch.

Even the American penchant for fantasy films and horror shows
was just another way of confronting death. Critic Rex Reed summarized the traditional psychoanalytic theory on this concept quite
concisely: "Horror movies, psychologists tell us, are just another

211

visual, vocal, and visceral way to tell we're alive. A scream a day keeps the doctor away.'' Horror films also sublimate fears of the undertaker. Dracula lives in a land of the undead. Frankenstein consists of resurrected parts and an electrical charge; in the modernist variant of this mad scientist fantasy, the life support systems in *Coma* (1978), the necrophagous vision of former Harvard physician Michael Crichton, promise organ transplants and longevity to the highest bidder.

Woody Allen proved the perfect comedian for the age of Thanatopsis: all this merrymaker's interviews began with bleak visions of transience. Allen's personal musings always seemed heavily laden with an angst that would make his idol Ingmar Bergman proud: "You have to deny the reality of death to go on everyday. But for me, even with all the distractions of my work and my life, I spend a lot of time face to face with my own mortality." The most highly lauded humorist of the decade reigned simultaneously as the crown prince of worry, despair, frustration, and inadequacy; his persona was Chaplin's tramp refurbished and ensnared in "the everlasting no" of *Sartor Resartus* and the "dark night of the soul" of Saint John of the Cross. Woody Allen played court jester to a dark age haunted by the plague of self-doubt, tossing his jests before a disgracefully pathetic monarch, and prancing madly for a court steeped in corruption and bloodied with foreign wars.

A 1970 Harris Poll revealed that two-thirds of the American population believed the country "had lost its national sense of direction" and that the system was so structured that "the rich get richer and the poor get poorer." A majority felt the United States was "on the verge of a national breakdown." Virtually no American institution could garner a majority vote of confidence. Given this collapse of the psychic underpinnings of American life, Woody Allen, the philosophical prankster, used traditional genres to structure his disturbing humor. Always a bird "without feathers," Allen was cagily "getting even" by circumventing the chaos, then exploiting the pandemonium with unsettling laughter.

Allen's commitment to genre and formula as a source of coherence is especially obvious in his wildly uneven early films. *Take the Money and Run* (1969), Allen's cops-and-robbers thriller, features a crook (Woody Allen) so dimwitted that no one at the bank can read his note.

Locked in prison, he does not aspire to the "top of the world, Ma";
Virgil Starkwell's parents clumsily hide their shame behind false
noses and comic glasses. None of the tried-and-true notions of depri-
vation and squalor explain this social misfit; he's mass murderer
Charles Starkweather without any panache. *Bananas* (1971) parodies
biographical films about revolutionary heroes, as a beleaguered product tester for an American conglomerate, Fielding Marshall (Allen)
stumbles into the leadership of a South American rebellion, only to
have newscaster Howard Cosell appear to provide detailed accounts
of his honeymoon and of a *coup d'état* by assassination. Marshall is
jostled by all the archvillains of the Seventies, the CIA, FBI, and
even J. Edgar Hoover himself; in an age of Pentagon papers, the meek
researcher turned militant is a hapless Daniel Ellsberg figure, over-
whelmed by events he cannot control. *Play It Again, Sam* (1972) is an
unabashed tribute to Bogart films, while *Everything You Always
Wanted to Know About Sex* (1972) uses David Reuben's book and the
rash of self-help best sellers as an excuse to string some memorable
skits together. Allen mocks television commercials about stomach
upset which use human characters to illustrate distress in a hilarious
reductio ad absurdum with he-man Burt Reynolds and cosmopolitan
charmer Tony Randall in the body's control room readying a cadre of
spermatozoa, including one reluctant participant in this "night journey" (Woody Allen), for an ejaculation. Understanding
psychotherapists are chided in Allen's delicious tale of a handsome,
gentle shrink (Gene Wilder) who tries to seduce the lamb that one of
his patients loves madly. And few serious horror pictures ever started
so magically as Allen's wondrous haunted house vignette, yet none
ended so uproariously as a runaway breast tries to nurse Allen to
death, only to be stymied by a gigantic brassiere. Both playboys and
bra-burners could relish the humor of this cinematic convention of
gigantism (borrowed from the age of momism) gone amuck.
Sleeper (1973), Woody Allen's slightly askew science-fiction film,
builds on the motif of gigantism with its oversized vegetables and its
precious nose waiting to be cloned into a new big brother. *Sleeper*
marks a new maturity for Allen as *cinéaste;* his one-liners about
Shanker and the bomb, the zillion hamburgers at McDonald's, and the
errors of former ages all mesh well with his daring sight gags, the
James Bond-like rocket-powered flights, the mechanized Jewish tailor

Woody Allen and Harold Gould in Allen's LOVE AND DEATH (1975).

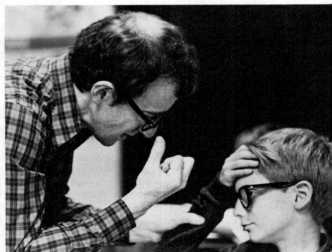

Woody Allen and Jonathan Munk in Allen's ANNIE HALL (1977).

shop, the pleasure machines, and the daring chases. *Sleeper* demonstrates an organic unity his earlier films desperately sought.

Love and Death (1975), Allen's sprawling version of a serious Russian philosophical novel as written by an inept scribbler with few ideas, satisfies more by wealth of incident and detail than by any sweeping design. It is both curious and mildly amusing to see Allen doing Russian dances, to hear him discourse about dueling, and to watch him klutz his way to fame and a chest full of medals. Diane Keaton makes a perfect Sonia, wrapped in furs and asleep in the arms of Boris (Allen). Even the outlandishly funny voice-overs and the rather literal walk with a white-sheeted symbolic death fit this stylish spoof, a *Mad* magazine version of *War and Peace*.

Allen's talent, however, would soon burst free from the narrow confines of sophomoric outlandishness, stylized satire, and genre parody. As Vincent Canby observed, Allen progressed so rapidly as a "major filmmaker" that audiences had to "pause occasionally" to catch their breath. *The Front* (1976) was such a pause for Allen himself; he took a serious dramatic role in a daring exposé of blacklisting in the entertainment business made by people who themselves had suffered its effects: director Martin Ritt, screenwriter Walter Bernstein, and star Zero Mostel. The film wears its politics as a proud star and builds to a grand moment of heroism when the once cowardly, apolitical Howard Prince (Woody Allen) tells an obviously prejudiced, senile, inquisitory congressional committee what he thinks of their superpatriotic meddling. Prince's triumphant and profane explosion probably marks the happiest moment for the Hollywood Ten and their supporters since the head of the House Un-American Activities Committee, the serpentine J. Parnell Thomas, went to prison for stealing government funds.

Allen's next film, *Annie Hall* (1977), was deeply autobiographical, yet it ranks as one of the most universally praised romantic comedies ever made; the deeper Allen probed the specifics of the love affair between Alvy Singer and Annie Hall (rather transparent fictional counterparts ot Woody Allen and Diane Keaton), the more it seemed he was limning the love affairs of all urban youth. *Annie Hall* offered a compendium of troubles in the single scene: the assassination fixation, the rock concerts, and the drug interludes; the spiders in the bathroom, the lobsters in the kitchen, and the traumas in growing up; the

215

tennis dates, the nightclub blues, and the familial horrors. *Annie Hall* vibrated with life (for all its allusions to death), tingled with romance (despite its constant worry about ennui), and ached with emotions (though it agonized over dissociation and frigidity). Woody Allen managed to maintain all these paradoxical balances largely by confronting them, admitting his inability to handle them, and then shrugging his shoulders as he sank his hands in his pocket. So what if Annie drives like a lunatic and her brother is a madman driving down a dark road? Ride along, worry like hell, but keep wisecracking in the face of death. Life may be insane, but, in the metaphor of Allen's principal joke, everyone needs the eggs.

Annie Hall won the Oscar for best picture in 1977, but Allen spent the night of the awards at New York's Michael's Pub, where chic urbanites pay five dollars a drink and more to hear him and his New Orleans Funeral Band play some mediocre jazz. It is not that Woody Allen does not huff and puff and take his music seriously; it is just that he is an extraordinary comedian and at best a sub-par clarinetist. Allen's *Interiors* (1978) also huffed and puffed a lot, but its music was equally strained, imitative, and mediocre. *Interiors*, a bleak film devoid of humor and wit, a plodding, self-consciously artistic film without one punch line or one joke, clearly demonstrated that, try as he may, Allen cannot be the Bergman or Antonioni of America; the skillful jester makes a dull and pretentious philosopher king.

Interiors is almost unbearably claustrophobic, pessimistic, despairing, and boring. Allen seems intent on bringing back all the existential angst of the late Fifties, the enervated characters, the pregnant pauses, and the studied, alienated décors. His film seems shot entirely under the dark cloud of nihilism. Most of his characters are so introspective, guilt-ridden, and self-centered that communication among them is totally impossible, as is any audience empathy. In *Interiors*, it is not so much that everything is presented through a glass darkly, but that the little there to be seen is so fragile, so evanescent, and so unimportant. There is an old Hollywood joke that Nestor Almendros "lights with firelight," William Fraker "lights with smoke," and that Allen's cameraman, Gordon Willis, "lights with available light"; in *Interiors*, that available light all comes in earthtones and beiges, cold as ice. Allen's much ado about nothing is indulgently scripted with what must be the most literary and unbelievable dialogue ever written and is filmed in a deliberately mannered style which constantly places intruding objects in the line of sight to obscure what little action there is to be seen.

The equally bizarre look of black-and-white Panavision heralded Allen's landmark comedy, *Manhattan* (1979), an exciting return to his real *métier*. *Manhattan* is, as its title proclaims, an exploration, celebration, and dissection of contemporary New York. The film is awash in cultural allusions best understood east of the Hudson and features a love story suited to Elaine's but not to Howard Johnson's. *Manhattan* actually manages to convince audiences that a forty-two-year-old mensch, played by Woody Allen, might find true happiness with an angelic eighteen-year-old innocent and that he could escape despair in the arms of a cerebral cherub with slightly damaged wings (Diane Keaton) while he remains buddies with her true love, his best friend (Michael Murphy).

All this romantic complexity counterpoints the philosophical questions Allen relentlessly probes. Allen is a laughing Sisyphus, but he makes sure everyone sees the rock, the hill, and the inevitable descent. Then and only then, like his mentor Bergman, Allen finds solace huddling together "in the middle of the night in a dark house." Allen's quick wit sparkles, but it never totally eclipses the serious themes he juggles so gracefully. The theme of *Manhattan*, Allen told interviewers, was "the problem of trying to live a decent life amidst all the junk of contemporary culture—the temptations, the seductions." In the face of that junk, the hero of *Manhattan*, Isaac Davis (Woody Allen), embraces some of the "greater glories" of civilization: Groucho Marx, Flaubert's *A Sentimental Education*, Cézanne's still lifes, Louis Armstrong's recording of "Potato Head Blues," and the second movement of Mozart's "Jupiter" symphony.

The Seventies' other great comedian, Mel Brooks, also found his "great glories" in the world of art, but he quickly gave them the full treatment with his own particular brand of custard pie in the face; Brooks's art is slapstick all the way. Vulgarity, exaggeration, and grotesquerie might well be his middle names. Both Mel Brooks and Woody Allen were major writers for Sid Caesar's *Your Show of Shows*, an innovative television series so far ahead of its time that its highlights could be exhibited theatrically decades later. Yet it is hard to conceive of more opposite styles: Allen is all reverence and reticence

217

Diane Keaton and Woody Allen in Allen's MANHATTAN (1979).

as he exploits popular art formulas, while Brooks is all energy and exhuberance as he explodes genres in his wild poetic conceits.

Brooks never goes for small touches and gentle laughter; it is full throttle all the time. "Springtime for Hitler" in *The Producers* (1968) is not wild enough a hyperbole for this comedic maniac; the production number has to be done by a freakish, hard-rocking, acid-head thug. In *The Twelve Chairs* (1970), based on a novel by renowned *littérateurs* Ilf and Petrov, the plot moves so quickly that soon no one can keep up with it, but no one cares. How could anyone resist the supplication of Otap Bender (Frank Langella), "I left an eye and a leg at the Winter Palace. Won't you leave something with me?"; or Dom DeLuise disguised as Father Fyodor and then as a gypsy on the run with a chair under his arm? As Brooks's colleague Gene Wilder so aptly described him, Mel Brooks is not a man at home with the hush of a Woody Allen; Brooks is the "loud kind of Jewish genius."

Blazing Saddles (1974), Brooks's best film and one of the most commercially successful film comedies of all time, was intended, Brooks told *New Yorker* interviewer-profiler Kenneth Tynan, as a "surrealist epic," an artistic rebuttal of the usual lies Hollywood told about the West: "I figured my career was finished anyway, so I wrote berserk, heartfelt stuff about white corruption and racism and Bible-thumping bigotry. . . . I just got everthing out of me—all my furor, my frenzy, my insanity, my love of life and hatred of death." Audiences flocked to this insane affirmation of dancing girls, Hollywood production numbers, stomach gas around the campfire, and gallows humor. Brooks had found the perfect vehicle for the age, and every year or so he could turn out his own mixture of homage and celebrity roast, his own reinterpretation of cinema's most revered traditions. *Young Frankenstein* (1974), for example, dresses up the beast (Peter Boyle) in coat and tails for a little soft-shoe, turns the kindly blindman (an inspired characterization by Gene Hackman) into a bumbling destroyer and works some ghastly comic howling around the role of Frau Blücher (Cloris Leachman). *Silent Movie* (1976), true to its title, depends on pratfall, mime, and old Keystone Kops antics to catapult audiences through an hour and a half with Mel Fun (Brooks), Marty Eggs (Marty Feldman), and Dom Bell (Dom DeLuise) as they confront the demented studio chief (Sid Caesar) and the forces of Engulf (Harold Gould) and Devour (Ron Carey). *High Anxiety* (1977), a

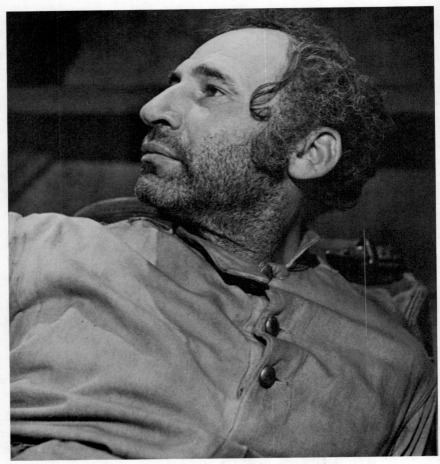

Mel Brooks in his THE TWELVE CHAIRS (1970).

Mel Brooks in his HIGH ANXIETY (1977).

Gene Wilder in Arthur Hiller's SILVER STREAK (1977).

homage to Hitchcock, merges the shower scene from *Psycho,* tons of droppings from *The Birds,* and the towers of *Vertigo* into one ecstatic thriller set in an institute for the "very, very nervous." Most of Brooks's humor is "very, very"; too much is never enough for this hyperactive talent. Excess is a Brooks hallmark.

Brooks's co-workers also saw the manifest opportunities for comedy in grotesque reinterpretation of popular movies, traditional heroes, and historical facts. Gene Wilder assayed the Victorian underground of Baker Street and its environs in *The Adventures of Sherlock Holmes's Smarter Brother* (1975), then headed West as the naïve Polish rabbi in *The Frisco Kid* (1979), who has an "Oy vey!" for every trouble. The bug-eyed Marty Feldman scoured the desert with the Foreign Legion in *The Last Remake of Beau Geste* (1977), then fleeced the lambs in *In God We Trust (Or Gimmie That Prime Time Religion),* which brought television personality Andy Kaufman to the screen. Brooks's friend and one-time sidekick, Carl Reiner, left *Your Show of Shows* for his own television career, and mastered his own brand of irreverence in the cult phenomenon, *Where's Poppa?* (1970), a lovely idyll of senility and attempted matricide, which included the infamous "tush" scene, and in the enormously popular *Oh God* (1977), an improbable coupling of a dull prophet (John Denver) and a grumpy, cigar-smoking vaudevillian trouper as deity (George Burns). Reiner's less successful *The One and Only* (1978) was an attempt to convert TV's the "Fonz" (Henry Winkler) into an ersatz Gorgeous George, frilly underwear and all.

The third principal writer for Sid Caesar's *Your Show of Shows* lacked both Woody Allen's intelligence and Mel Brooks's braggadocio, yet he did manage to become the most prolific and consistently successful humorist on Broadway. Neil Simon's comedies are never as inspired or weighty as Allen's masterpieces and they are never as frenetic and side-splitting as Brooks's madcap antics, yet they are uniformly craftsmanlike and well structured. They extract chuckles quite professionally with all the finesse of a skilled dentist who knows just the right amount of novocaine to use to avoid pain without numbing all the patient's senses.

Simon, the master of the *bon mot* and one-liner, followed wherever audiences led him. If the mood was President Ford's infamous "Drop dead" to New York, Simon could chide big-city foibles *(The Out of*

George Segal and Ruth Gordon in Carl Reiner's WHERE'S POPPA (1970).

Towners, 1970) and lacerate Gotham City's insanities (*The Prisoner of Second Avenue*, 1975) without losing a sense of its special pleasures and ambience (*The Goodbye Girl*, 1978). When nostalgia for yesterday's showmen (*The Sunshine Boys*, 1975) or bygone heroes (*Murder by Death*, 1976) or the old genres (*The Cheap Detective*, 1978) was in vogue, Simon could supply the necessary cute situations, exaggerated personalities, and campy dialogue. When the East lost prominence to the West, Simon could go from uptight to laid back, from tense to mellow, from the *Plaza Suite* (1971) to the *California Suite* (1978). And when autobiographical romantic comedies became the rage, Neil Simon was ready with *Chapter Two* (1979), starring spouse Marsha Mason in the story of their whirlwind romance and subsequent marital tensions. Never at a loss for lines guaranteed to generate laughs, Simon was the toastmaster of the Seventies, discreet, only slightly pompous, always insubstantial, but pleasant enough to be endured.

If the writers from Sid Caesar's *Your Show of Shows* shaped comedy for most of the Seventies, the performers on the most original television program of the decade, *Saturday Night Live*, pointed the way to the Eighties. Star John Belushi helped make *National Lampoon Animal House* (1978) a runaway hit with scores of imitators; studios took one look at the grosses generated by the toga parties, food riots, panty raids, and fraternity pranks of this adolescent Marx Brothers fantasy, and they quickly commissioned outlandish comedies so long as they were youth oriented and pointedly topical. Imports like *Saturday Night Live* regular Bill Murray's *Meatballs* (1979) and innovative recyclings of material rejected by television censors, like *Mondo Video* (1979), demonstrated that the proper youthful outlook could compensate for many technical shortcomings. After all, the laughably bad production of *Up in Smoke* (1978) did little to deter Cheech and Chong fans; studios were bidding millions for the right to make this team of inarticulate dopers the new Abbott and Costello of the cocaine age. Meanwhile, Steven Spielberg spent millions on *1941*, a film that depended a great deal on the popularity of *Saturday Night Live* alumni Dan Aykroyd and John Belushi. Another cast member from this celebrated comedy series, Albert Brooks, did his own satire on television's most famous family, the Louds, who had been the subject of Craig Gilbert's twelve-hour documentary for PBS in 1973, *An American Family*, an ambitious undertaking that

225

raised real questions about the need for privacy, the rights of a documentary maker, and humanity's ability to deal with the naked truths of life in the modern age. In Brooks's *Real Life* (1978), the story behind this *cinéma verité* invasion of the suburbs involves small-town boosterism and corruption, media politics, and an artist's ego. In the end, everything goes up in flames, but there is some hope for the survivors of this holocaust.

The rash of anarchic, youth-oriented comedies treating adult themes confirmed Samuel Z. Arkoff's dictum that "the more downbeat the real world looks, the more the public buys upbeat movies." Television's so-called "late night" entertainment, the sophisticated banter about sexual hangups, political infighting, and the collapse of the economy, the blackout skits about betrayal, adultery, and divorce, the witty repartee concerning current affairs, celebrity peccadilloes, and contemporary fads—once the staple of talk shows and variety hours—drew a world-weary group of adolescents to theaters where no holds were barred and more than seven dirty words could be uttered with impunity. Joan Rivers could drown infants, parody the Nativity, and mock all nationalities in *Rabbit Test* (1977), a vitriolic portrait of a man who had a baby, played by television personality Billy Crystal, the homosexual regular on the iconoclastic series *Soap*. Richard Pryor's hilarious ethnic humor, replete with four-letter words, could be filmed live in concert, time and again; and the rotund Allan Funt could ask (then show and tell) *What Do You Say to a Naked Lady?* (1970). The British Monty Python team even approached what many called blasphemy in their *Life of Brian* (1979), a jaundiced portrait of a scurrilous rogue born in the stable next to Christ's, raised by a mercenary hag, and then crucified to the chords of a cheerful little ditty about the pleasures of life.

Not all Seventies comedies were, of course, so scandalous, and not all of the decade's humor was tied to serious themes. Elaine May tried her hand at a screwball comedy (*A New Leaf*, 1971) and at a bland romantic adventure (*The Heartbreak Kid*, 1972). George Hamilton gave a *tour de force* performance as a bored Dracula in *Love at First Bite* (1979), sulking in heavy accents about the tedium and humiliations of the vampiric lifestyle: "Do you know what it's like to go around for seven hundred years dressed like a head waiter?" And for what seemed like eternity, Peter Sellers resurrected the Pink Panther in an endless stream of "returns" and "revenges." By decade's end, however, even an egoist like Sellers could see the need for more cerebral undertakings, and he starred in the long-awaited filming of Jerzy Kosinski's viciously sardonic novel *Being There*, a gripping and hilarious dissertation on the role media play in shaping man's destiny, and a penetrating character study of Herbert Marcuse's one-dimensional man stripped of even the barest remnants of control.

Comedy provided a major outlet for serious writers and directors in the Seventies, an escape hatch from the blockbuster mentality and the sequel syndrome haunting Hollywood. As Woody Allen explained the phenomenon to Kenneth Tynan in casual conversation, people who "do comedy are traditionally left alone. The studious feel we're on a wavelength that's alien to them. They believe we have access to some secret formula that they don't. With drama, it's different. Everybody thinks he's an expert." This arrogant assumption of expertise frequently closed studio doors to serious filmmakers, who had to finance cerebral projects with independent funds or through tax shelters; then, with or without studio support in the production stages, conscientious filmmakers frequently found themselves with no outlet for their films, with no place to showcase projects distinguished by intelligence, not violence, and with no means of distribution. Independent distributor David Baughn summarized the prevailing Hollywood view of serious and artistic cinema quite aptly in a September 1979 *Filmmakers* interview: "Generally speaking, the mass audience doesn't go to the movies for an intellectual experience and they don't want to search out a special film; they want an entertainment that is easily understood and has no problems to be solved. Filmmakers more interested in money than fame should remember this and consider it a rule."

Because of the problems serious cinema faced in a commercial market, the major film festivals became important testing grounds for new product, arenas that could provide both fame and some support from the film industry. Gifted filmmakers might win prizes like the Gold Palm or Silver Bear and lure a distributor into gambling that a *succès d'estime* might also become a box-office bonanza. Cannes, Berlin, Locarno, Venice, Sorrento, Toronto, and other cities around

227

the globe became capitals of film art and film marketing; in the United States, Chicago, Los Angeles, and New York make their own efforts to offer suitable exposure to difficult but distinguished films.

A typical festival film like James Frawley's *Kid Blue* (1973), for example, which featured sterling performances by Dennis Hopper and Warren Oates, needed more special attention and more careful handling than Twentieth Century-Fox eventually gave it. Henry Jaglom's *A Safe Place* (1971) received similarly unsuitable handling from Columbia Pictures, who were unable to capitalize on the mystique of Orson Welles and the popular appeal of Tuesday Weld and Jack Nicholson. Howard Zieff's charming *Hearts of the West* (1975) slipped through United Artists' hands so quickly that few television viewers knew the re-edited version they saw had ever been shown theatrically. Jonathan Demme's *Handle with Care* (1977), also known in a longer version as *Citizens Band*, an insightful and complex comedy about CB radio operators, their dreams and fixations, their identity crises and infidelities, perplexed Paramount's publicity staff so much that they sponsored a round of free exhibitions that packed audiences in yet failed to generate enough "word of mouth" from one "good buddy" to another "good buddy" to keep this film from quickly going "down and out." Director Demme had gotten his start, like so many adventurous filmmakers, with Roger Corman, the reigning king of B movies, working on a women's prison film, *Caged Heat* (1974), which managed to make a number of salient points on women's liberation even as it exploited nudity to pack male patrons in. Despite the debacle with *Handle with Care*, Demme's obvious directorial gifts were soon employed again on *The Last Embrace* (1979), an intriguing homage to Hitchcock, and Demme's career seemed destined to blossom in the Eighties.

Festivals also premiered a good number of major undertakings by well-known directors who were trying something a little different. John Huston, for example, brought his adaptation of Flannery O'Connor's *Wise Blood* (1979), a scorching look at repression and the revival racket, to the international circuit. The Seventies proved quite kind to this poet of masculinity and shattered hopes; both his trenchant portrait of a boxer on the skids, *Fat City* (1972), and his long-delayed version of Rudyard Kipling's novella *The Man Who Would Be King* (1975) proved worthy successors to his earlier masterpieces.

Stacy Keach in John Huston's FAT CITY (1972).

Huston knew how to mix adventure and insight; he was the American master of downbeat cinematic parables.

The Czech master of upbeat realistic miniatures, Milos Forman, immediately after he emigrated to America (largely on the strength of festival successes abroad), created a devilishly perceptive comedy about the generation gap in the United States, *Taking Off* (1971), that played foreign festivals but somehow got lost in the shuffle of American film marketing. Lavishly praised elsewhere, this macabre romp through open casting calls in Greenwich Village, pot parties for confused parents, and strip poker nights with the Geritol set, was scripted in part by the strange pairing of John Guare and Jean-Claude Carrière, and the film featured a well-modulated performance by Buck Henry as the disillusioned father of a runaway daughter who finally recognizes that "She's out there having fun. That's what we ought to do—go some place and have fun, goddammit." Another émigré Czech director, Ivan Passer, who was represented at the New York Film Festival by *Born to Win* (1971), died before he fully understood the American idiom, but his idiosyncratic Seventies enterprises, including *Law and Disorder* (1974) and *Crime and Passion* (1976), evidenced considerable intelligence despite their obvious gaucheries. Both Robert Mulligan's *Bloodbrothers* (1977) and James Ivory's *Roseland* (1977) also had quite embarrassing moments, but they did evidence their creators' unique commitment to a complex presentation of sophisticated realities and to both intellectual and aesthetic subtlety in the face of market pressures.

The equally committed and talented director Joan Micklin Silver, who burst on the artistic scene with one of the most accomplished first features ever, *Hester Street* (1974), a bemusing study of immigrant travails and cultural adaptation among young Jews on New York's lower East Side, had her short film, *Bernice Bobs Her Hair* (1976), based on F. Scott Fitzgerald's story and originally produced for the highly praised PBS TV anthology *The American Short Story,* chosen for participation in the New York Film Festival. She then went on to make two other important features in the Seventies, directing *Between the Lines* (1977), a quirky recapitulation of the Sixties as reflected in the lives of a scruffy group of reporters who watch their underground newspaper prosper, only to change radically; and then producing her husband's *On the Yard* (1978), a realistic vision of life

Lynn Carlin and Audra Lindley in Milos Forman's TAKING OFF (1971).

on "the inside," based on Malcolm Braly's prison novel, and stunningly photographed by Alan Metzger, one of the most adept of a whole new generation of cinematographers who got their start in commercials. Silver's *Head Over Heels* (1979) proved, however, a dull interpretation of Ann Beattie's difficult novel, *Chilly Scenes of Winter,* and received little exposure.

Many quite laudable and accomplished American film projects could have profited from the prestige and exposure international festivals lent to serious productions. A major award could often open markets that otherwise were either totally inaccessible, or, in most cases, not sufficiently presold. Festival publicity often made the difference between notoriety and obscurity; a major award often boosted the sales of tickets the way a designer label escalated the price of jeans. Without the "hype" of officially recognized and lauded artistic excellence, some fine film projects garnered but meager box-office returns. Philip Kaufman, for example, saw two of his most daring projects almost completely ignored: his gritty Western, *The Great Northfield Minnesota Raid* (1971), a highly imaginative reconstruction of the James gang's exploits and the inevitable industrialization sweeping the West, and *The White Dawn* (1974), an ambitious and thoughtful study of cultural clashes in the Arctic. Barbara Loden watched *Wanda* (1971), her original portrait of a woman trapped in an endless cycle of want, crime, complicity, and loneliness, vanish despite many fine critical reviews. Other projects—Claudia Weill's *Girlfriends* (1977), an understated, underfunded picture of a female photographer's search for companionship and independence; Ridley Scott's *The Duellists* (1977), an accomplished reconstruction of Conrad's thematically rich study of horror and personal dignity; Brian De Palma's *Obsession* (1976), a cinematic hall of mirrors celebrating Hitchcock and his craft; and John Carpenter's *Assault on Precinct 13* (1976), an American *ciné-roman* scripted in dark blacks and bloody reds—were all films that failed to generate enough interest to intrigue the mass audience.

Some other notable projects that never managed to find the recognition nor the popularity they deserved include a film that did well in European festivals but poorly at home, Billy Wilder's *Fedora* (1978), a flawed but provocative working of *Sunset Boulevard* that vents his spleen about "the kids with beards" who have taken over Hollywood;

232

Paul Sylbert's *The Steagle* (1971), a Wiz Kid's odyssey in the America of small minds and narrow opinions; William Richert's *Winter Kills* (1979), a Richard Condon *roman à* Kennedy full of nihilistic good spirits; Monte Hellman's *Two Lane Blacktop* (1972), a good film possibly destroyed by its own excessive concern for indirection and ambiguity; and Frank Perry's *Diary of a Mad Housewife* (1971), a critical document evidencing a burgeoning women's liberation movement.

Ralph Bakshi, a new-wave animator, also created interesting documents about modern foibles in his irreverent, X-rated sketches *Fritz the Cat* (1973), *Heavy Traffic* (1973), and *Coonskin* (1975). Bakshi found his audience, however, only when he prepared mature and captivating ventures into the dark realms of magic (*Wizards,* 1977) and through the well-cataloged Middle Earth of *The Lord of the Rings* (1978). Bakshi's extravagant and somewhat incoherent introduction to Tolkien's trilogy stunned industry pundits by capturing unexpectedly grand box-office returns. Middle Earth and Froda suited the age of fantasy; its epic wars and grand quests were majestic alternatives to everyday life in America.

As wild-eyed fantasies prospered, however, the opposite fate waited documentary makers; the apostles of filming real people in real-life situations had but limited success in the Seventies. Tabloid celebrity features like the Maysles Brothers' *Grey Gardens* (1975), an ill-advised, embarrassing peek at two of Jackie Onassis' oldest and poorest relatives who obviously trusted the film makers' discretion more than they should have, made minor headway in the American market, but major exhibitors and the popular audience seemed oblivious to fine works like Haskell Wexler's *Brazil: A Report on the Torture* (1971), Emile De Antonio's *Underground* (1977), and Howard Smith's *Marjoe* (1972). Even Peter Davis's topical *Hearts and Minds* (1974), one of the few cinematic visions of Vietnam, was refused distribution by Columbia Pictures; Warner Brothers released it only when Henry Jaglom arranged a lucrative tax shelter package. When *Hearts and Minds* won the Oscar for best documentary, it achieved the attention it deserved largely because Bert Schneider, in accepting the award, read a message to the American people from the Provisional Revolutionary Government of South Vietnam.

Schneider's action was denounced as arrogant and irrational; he

233

Necron 99 in Ralph Bakshi's WIZARDS (1977).

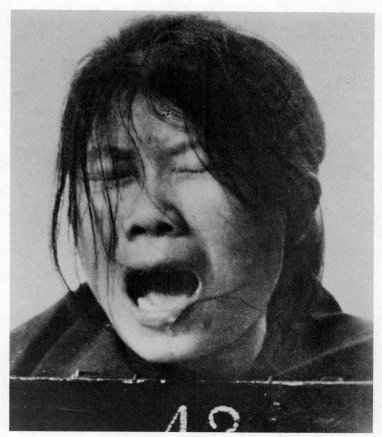

Peter Davis' HEARTS AND MINDS (1974).

was assailed from many quarters and bore the brunt of the attack in Bo Burlingham's pointed combination of fact and fiction, "Politics Under the Palms," published in *Esquire* and later reprinted in James Monaco's *Media Culture*. Burlingham's main focus was trendy leftist posturing in Hollywood but, like so many Hollywood stories, his article soon centered on a death, the bizarre asphyxiation of Artie Ross, who died strapped to a tank of nitrous oxide. As Burlingham notes, most of Ross's friends ruled out suicide; he left no note and he had not been depressed. He had merely been seeking a new high, risking a new trip, running from death only to find it. With chilling irony, Burlingham then cites Paul Williams' response to this tragedy: "Then he shrugged. 'Well, we know this much,' he said. 'Artie Ross died laughing.'"

8. Darkness on the Edge of Town

> *During the 1960's, the place to start changing the culture was Harvard University. But in the 1980's that place will be the Sunset Strip. I feel the direction of the future will come from Hollywood. . . .*
> TIMOTHY LEARY

IN APRIL 1979, soothsayer-savant Vincent Canby startled the urbane readers of the Sunday *New York Times* "Leisure Section" with a portentous lead-in to a routine assessment of the latest Oscar telecast: "The American motion picture industry is a large lump in the belly of the python called television. Most of the time one doesn't notice this." Canby's jungle metaphor is particularly apt, though he might well have extended it to include the other flora and fauna in this overheated, "red in tooth and claw" tropics: the record companies, the commercial theaters, the publishing houses, the newspapers and magazines, the cable television systems, and the consumer electronics factories, which make up the brave new world of entertainment conglomerates. In the Seventies, all forms of leisure, from bowling alleys to fast-food franchises, from drive-ins to hi-fi stores, and from disco to designer jeans, were merging into one gargantuan business, monopolized by a handful of multinational corporations, integrated seemingly both horizontally and vertically. Beverly Hills, Burbank, Motown, New York, and Hollywood were mere pushpins in a larger globe, and a new sign atop Mount Lee could never restore the old autonomy. Movies, television, records, and print were quietly merging into one cash-flow statistic on an interlocking ledger. Tinseltown was, once and for all, a minor suburb to the megalopolis of money stretching across the continent and finally around the world.

Movie fans were, of course, horrified at the implications of cinema becoming just another "lump in the belly" of these communications-recreation empires. James Monaco in his study of *American Film Now* (1979) warned quite perspicaciously: "Reading the corporate annual reports of the film companies and their conglomerate owners,

237

you get the feeling that if theatrical films disappeared within the next five years all of them would survive rather nicely." Banker George Bruns, assistant vice-president of the First National Bank of Boston, the principal lending institution for Warner Brothers, Fox, and Columbia, was more sanguine about the very same prospect in a September 1976 *Film Comment* interview, when he praised major studios for pushing film to the periphery: "If their movies were totally unsuccessful, they could get along nicely. These major companies have built other operations generally related to the entertainment-type business—broadcasting, publishing, records, music publishing, and so forth."

Even individual company heads, in fact, began by the end of the decade to speculate on the demise of traditional forms of exhibition, foreseeing the possibility that all America might soon witness its "last picture show." Gone forever might well be the first-run houses and the "nabes," the ushers and the popcorn, the double features and the art house; and in their place, the new videocassette decks, the videodiscs, the wall-size televisions, the direct satellite to home broadcasts, three-dimensional and stereophonic television, and laser-fiber-optics-holographic entertainment right out of *Star Wars*. Corporate presidents like Steven J. Ross of Warner Communications could attempt to assure stockholders and to dispel the gloom attendant on the death of traditional movies with his bold declaration that "whatever the means of transmission, we're ready and able to supply the product." By 1979 Warners already had gone into videotape and videodisc, as well as establishing a home video-game division, a cable enterprise, several publishing divisions, software companies, and a major record label. Paramount was leasing films in cassette form through Fotomat, and Columbia was working with Time-Life on a mail-order scheme.

One major impetus for these new directions in marketing was the success of the record industry in the Seventies. It captured the hearts, minds, and dollars of the younger audience, the very audience films aimed at, and actually surpassed the revenues of the film industry. Industry pundits could not ignore the fact that the album of *Saturday Night Fever* grossed almost four times what the film did. Revenues from soundtracks became so important in the Seventies that some films, like *Sgt. Peppers' Lonely Hearts Club Band* (1978), *Grease*

238

Daniel Ades in Dennis Hopper's THE LAST MOVIE (1971).

(1978), and *Hair* (1979), were more concert performances of hit albums than anything else. Even major artistic successes like *Nashville* (1975) often owed their very existence to their musical themes; screenwriter Joan Tewkesbury told many interviewers that the film came about "because the studio had an idea that, even if the movie didn't make any money, it could get rich off the soundtrack album." Whenever possible, Seventies movies featured either a rock star or at least some marketable music. Even Dennis Hopper's prophetic *The Last Movie* (1971), an offbeat homage to Samuel Fuller, featured the music of Kris Kristofferson; Floyd Mutrux' quirky *Aloha, Bobby and Rose* (1975) gyrated to the phenomenally popular ballads of Elton John; and many older critics thought Hal Ashby undercut the effect of *Coming Home* (1978) with an obtrusive collage of well-known rock classics, including the legendary "Sympathy with the Devil."

As the record industry moved closer to both film and television, the three enterprises virtually coalesced. As a result, the lines between material that could only be experienced in a theater and product intended for home consumption became ever more tenuous. Traditional film exhibitors were all but squeezed out of the action; the regular moviegoer was becoming an anomaly. First-run movies, even the most successful blockbusters, went from exclusive showings to network broadcast with startling speed; the theatrical hits of the early Seventies became the routine television fare of the late Seventies. *The Godfather* saga, for example, which did landslide business in 1972 and 1974, had barely ended its final sub-run when it was broadcast in 1977 as "the complete novel for television," a nine-hour extravaganza supposedly personally reshaped by Coppola himself, which was touted as being broader in scope than the theatrical film. *Jaws* (1975), which was rereleased in 1978, became a "Sunday special" for NBC in 1979. More than original films were shown on television, however. Sometimes the python made an elaborate banquet out of a particularly juicy lump. A landmark film like Robert Altman's *M*A*S*H* (1970), for example, might inspire a whole comic series loosely based on its characters. The anarchic, anti-establishment, irreverent black comedy was laundered for the mass taste; the cast and director were changed, but the name endured for almost ten years, until it was possible in one week in New York to view on television the original film, prime-time original episodes, and syndicated reruns late at night.

Keith Carradine and Geraldine Chaplin in Robert Altman's NASHVILLE (1975).

Successful films like *National Lampoon's Animal House* might generate a whole rash of television imitators like *Brothers and Sisters, Delta House, Co-ed Fever,* and others. *American Graffiti* (1973) was the progenitor for home-screen successes like *Happy Days* and *Laverne and Shirley*, and even the classy *Alice Doesn't Live Here Anymore* (1975) spawned offspring like *Alice*. Larry White, the president of Columbia Television, told Aljean Hermetz of the *New York Times* that "television audiences have an appetite for ingratiating, appealing characters"; thus *Julia* (1977), *The Turning Point* (1977), *The Cheap Detective* (1978), *California Suite* (1978), and many others were all being considered for further development as television series. And the flow was not all from film to television, either. *Battlestar Galactica* (1978), an overpriced science fiction series was re-edited into a feature film, and *Buck Rogers in the Twenty-fifth Century* (1979) flashed back and forth from one medium to the other. Made-for-television movies, once the bastard child of the film industry, had by mid-decade replaced the B movies of the past. In 1974, for example, 118 first-run theatrical features played network television, but there were also over 130 new telefilms. And in 1978, *Elvis,* a made-for-television feature, proved more popular than both a rerun of *Gone with the Wind* and the television premiere of the best picture of 1975, *One Flew Over the Cuckoo's Nest*. The evolution of telefilms in the Seventies would cast new light on the thesis Jerzy Toeplitz espoused in his *Hollywood and After: The Changing Face of Movies in America* (1974). Toeplitz acutely noted: "In 1955 live television accounted for eighty-four percent of the total; fifteen years later, in 1970, for only five percent. This technological transformation of live prerecorded television in the late Fifties saved Hollywood from certain liquidation." What Toeplitz did not foresee is exactly Vincent Canby's vision: the motion picture industry swallowed alive by television. Motion picture studios in the Seventies avoided liquidation by being "engulfed and devoured."

Surely the most distressing evidence that movies and television are inextricably linked comes each year at Oscar time in Los Angeles. Members of the Academy are invited to see all the nominees free at studio screenings, but even these free exhibitions do not have the appeal that Channel Z and other pay cable stations do. As a result, many nominated films play the cable with the studios making special

*Jack Nicholson in Milos Forman's ONE FLEW OVER THE CUCKOO'S
NEST (1975).*

243

pricing and leasing concessions to display their best products via subscription television and hopefully to garner the needed votes for an Oscar.

All media in the Seventies seem to be merging in one great bath of image and myth. The victims in the "Son of Sam" case rushed to sell their stories before David Berkowitz could profit, as columnist Jimmy Breslin peddled his .44 caliber murder mystery to paperback houses. guzzled light beer on television, and inspired the characterization of the journalist hero in *Slow Dancing in the Big City* (1978), itself a spinoff destined for quick sale to cable systems, largely because of the resurgence in the interest in dance generated by *The Turning Point* (1977). Virtually no contemporary phenomenon escaped exploitation. Patty Hearst, the kidnapped scion of a publishing family, proved the hostage of television, magazines, and films, and finally a victim of overexposure. Watergate generated best sellers, movies, records, lecture tours, television specials, and videocassettes.

In this all-encompassing media bath, conglomerate executives searched for the marketing strategy and development program that would maximize profits. The theatrical film was merely one possible avenue to the mass audience and consumer market. Sunset Boulevard was just one of the many highways corporate America explored to reach the pursestrings of the nation. More often than not, conglomerates used radio, television, films, publishing, and merchandising in tandem. In 1979, for example, 131 million dollars were spent for advertising current theatrical films on television. And this did not take into account the special "wrap party" broadcasts for films like *Saturday Night Fever,* the cross-pollination involved in television shows like *The Muppets Go Hollywood,* an unabashed commercial for *The Muppet Movie* (1979), or the constant hours of chatter on late-night talk shows. Critic William Paul may well have discerned an important truth in his perceptive article "Hollywood Harakiri" (*Film Comment,* March 1977), when he observed that, "If television was a competitor to anything, it was to the movie theaters themselves, and the movie producing companies no longer had corporate ties to them." Entertainment conglomerates have steadfastly avoided re-involvement in the exhibition end of the business, avoiding antitrust litigation, and perhaps keying on the Eighties when, as Hans Fantel observed, the living room may be "a primary showplace for the performing arts."

Crystal-ball gazing, is, of course, a dangerous business, especially when emerging technology constantly multiplies the possibilities. Some evidence exists, however, to suggest that the growth of the entertainment-leisure-recreation segment of the American economy could mean increased vigor and health for all its components. Competition among various media might actually result in a considerably bigger pie to be divided; each success could boost the appeal of all its competitors. Audiences who enjoy one show or film may well come back for more and more. When the Disney Studio, for example, sued Sony to bar the sale of videocassette recorders because of potential copyright violations, a landmark suit decided for the defendant and evidence was introduced to show that twenty-five percent of the recorder owners were watching more broadcast television after they acquired their recording units. Other evidence showed that almost eighty-five percent of these video buffs claimed they attended movies with the same or even greater frequency after their purchase of a recorder.

Audience demographics also augur well for the continued viability of conventional exhibition. In 1979, nearly ninety percent of the admissions at cinema were persons twelve to forty, and nearly thirty percent of admissions were patrons between the age of sixteen and twenty. These teenagers and young people will always need a place to congregate outside the cloistered confines of home and family. The future of Hollywood may then not merely be a function of the jungle ethic. The fittest may prosper, but all forms of entertainment may survive. Evolution, however, will be the rule, not the exception. As John Howkins illustrates in his provocative *Sight and Sound* article "Television May Never be the Same Again" (published in the summer of 1979), none of the old verities may hold; free television will be reshaped by pay arrangements and those in turn will be reshaped by original materials on disc and tape. Howkins suggests, however, an emerging pattern to all media distribution, "from the smallest and richest audiences to the larger mass audience." Film, which began in America as the poor man's escape, the immigrant's respite from drudgery, may well become, at least in its theatrical exhibitions, a rich man's art or the plaything of adolescents.

The onset of the Eighties is a time of great promise and peril for Hollywood. The challenge of the new technologies recalls the problems

Cybill Shepherd and Timothy Bottoms in Peter Bogdanovich's THE LAST PICTURE SHOW (1971).

poised in the Fifties by television. At that time, Samuel Goldwyn warned Garson Kanin that shortsighted studio heads were "gonna kill the whole business." The real secret, Goldwyn felt, was to use "the box," the new technology, to bring money back to filmmakers. His words, recorded by Kanin in his best seller *Hollywood*, may hold the key to the survival of film making in America: "The box is just a distribution business. That's all. We're going to have to figure out some way to use it, but to use it like a *distribution* business. Not to sell some goddam toothpaste, f' Chrissake."

Index

250

254

258